Woodstock
dream

Woodstock

Elliott Landy

dream

 teNeues

For this edition:
© 2000 te Neues Verlag GmbH, Kempen
For the original edition:
© 1999 Federico Motta Editore S.p.A., Milan
All rights reserved.
For the photographs:
© 1999 Elliott Landy, in Italy represented by
Agenzia Grazia Neri

To contact Elliott Landy
E-Mail: go@landyvision.com
Website: http://www.landyvision.com

Original book title:
Woodstock Dream. Elliott Landy

English translation: Louise Müller
German translation: Theresa-M. Bullinger
Production: Wallstein Verlag GmbH, Göttingen

Die Deutsche Bibliothek – CIP-Einheitsaufnahme
Ein Titeldatensatz für diese Publikation ist bei
der Dcutschen Bibliothek erhältlich

ISBN 3-8238-5452-6
Printed in Italy

Contents / Inhalt

The Eternal Dream

The following words appeared in the 24th December 1965 edition of the renowned American weekly magazine „Time": „FBI statistics show that young people under 25 years of age account for 73.4 per cent of crimes such as murder, rape, theft and other serious offences; they are to blame for 31 per cent of all fatal accidents. Young people organize demonstrations for the enemies of our country. Young people go on marches, bearing banners with offensive or abusive slogans... And the latest of their activities seems to be the founding of 'free universities', where they can study, so they say, subjects not taught at traditional universities – topics such as 'true sexual experience' and 'the revelations of hallucinogens'. The young men look like girls, the girls are like men, their protest songs are endless prophecies of the terrible things they claim will happen in this society, a society they see as spending twelve billion dollars a year on cars, guitars, anti-acne lotion, shampoo and more and more extravagant clothing."

This was the voice of fundamentalist America in the Sixties. Two years before, in Dallas, the country had witnessed the death of its President John Kennedy as the victim of an ambush, and only three years later the murder of the 1964 Nobel Prize-winner Martin Luther King and Robert Kennedy, John's brother, who was a sure candidate to win the November presidential elections instead of the Republican candidate Richard Nixon. Some months before the article appeared in „Time", Lyndon Johnson, Kennedy's Vice-President, was officially nominated President of the United States of America. Shortly after the elections, under the pretence of fleet incidents in the Gulf of Tongking, Johnson began air raids on North Vietnam. In the United States people started saying – we voted for Johnson and got Goldwater in the White House (Goldwater, his rival in the elections, was a man with extreme right-wing political beliefs, who advocated racial segregation).

This was the social and political background against which the dream of the Woodstock generation was born.

Elliott Landy, who shot the photographs for this book, said to me: „The world seemed so dumb … to make people change, I thought it was enough to take photos of the world and to show people how dumb it is (or how beautiful and creative it could be). For ridiculous reasons and out of some kind of false patriotic sentiment the United States had got stuck in the tunnel of a terrible war in Vietnam. So towards the end of 1967 I left Denmark (where I was working as a stills photographer on a movie set) and went back to the USA with the express intention of working to stop the Vietnam war by taking photographs of the big peace demos in Washington and New York."

The Vietnam war was one of the first degenerate wars in the latter part of our century. On 16th September 1966, Arturo Jemolo wrote the following words in the „Stampa": „In the wars of antiquity, soldiers plundered towns and killed and raped civilians. But these were regular soldiers, a profession not likely to be chosen by good Christians. And plunder and rape did not fall under the call of duty. But in the last wars of our time soldiers have actually been under command to sink merchant ships, giving their crews not a chance of survival; soldiers have been given orders to shoot at civilians from the air and to aim flame projectors at inhabited buildings. The destruction of towns with bombs has become a normal act of war". It was photographs by people like Larry Barrows, Nick Ut and Dan McCullin that brought these kind of atrocities to the American public eye.

Elliott Landy had no desire to become a war photographer in Vietnam: „I don't want to end up being killed or maimed by a bomb", he said.

During this period, he immersed himself in the world of music.

„If I hadn't loved the music, I wouldn't have been able to take the photos. The fascination of the musicians at that time lay in their completely individual way of making music, inspired by the most secret, deep, intimate and poetic depths of their souls. The way they organized their concerts was completely new – they didn't just perform, they communicated with the boys and girls in the audience, got them up to dance, encouraged them to change their way of life and become part of a big community based on peace and love.

In 1968 I was at one of the big psychedelic concerts at the Anderson Theater in New York Village and Fillmore East with Jimi Hendrix, Jim Morrison, Chuck Berry, and at the Newport Folk Festival with Joan Baez, Pete Seeger, Janis Joplin and in Woodstock. It completely changed my life and my way of taking photographs. Taking photos of the singers became a kind of obsession, as though I had fallen victim to ecstasy."

Elliott Landy was an official Woodstock photographer and one of the few photographers allowed on stage during the legendary concerts. He shot some outstanding photographs capturing the mood of this memorable era, and is considered to be one of its most ‚authentic' witnesses. He designed covers for „Life", „Newsweek" and „Rolling Stone" on the theme of the Woodstock generation. He was the designer of the record cover for *Nashville Skyline* by Bob Dylan and some of the albums by The Band. Some of his photos are quite unforgettable – Jim Morrison looking like a Piero della Francesca angel or Janis Joplin in concert at the Anderson Theater (her face reminds us of Eve's fall from paradise in Masaccio's fresco). Not to mention the concert shots on stage using infrared film – truly disturbing pictures reminiscent of the works of Basquiat – or the quiet portraits of Bob Dylan in his apartment in Woodstock.

Young people were the co-stars of the Woodstock era, moving like waves in time to the storm of the music. These young people, described by the Berkeley Sociology professor Edgar Friedenberg as the true heirs of American Puritanism, had a dream – they wanted to change the world they had grown up in by campaigning against war, by fighting for a fair share of civil rights for black Americans, and by refusing to accept „the democratic serfdom of the advanced industrial civilisation" (as defined by Marcuse).

To quote Landy again: „In this battle of ideals they chose musicians as their leaders, but in my opinion, they made one mistake. These artists really could get young people carried away and give them a revolutionary cultural experience that lifted them out of the mist of fear. But as individuals these same artists had, on the whole, experienced tragic and self-destructive things. Dylan himself told me quite clearly that he didn't want to be a leader, all he wanted to do was communicate a kind of poetic feeling."

In this context, Furio Colombo reminds us of Dylan's famous interview in „Playboy" in 1966. Here are some excerpts from this interview, where he answers the question of why he had stopped composing and singing songs with a clear message, i.e. political and protest songs:

„I've stopped composing and singing anything that has either a reason to be written or a motive to be sung. ... 'Protest' is not my word. The word ‚protest', I think, was made up for people undergoing surgery. ... Anyway, message songs, as everybody knows, are a drag. It's only single girls under 14 that could possibly have time for them...
– In their admiration for you, many young people have begun to imitate the way you dress – which one adult commentator has called 'self-consciously oddball and defiantly sloppy' ...

... I know the fellow that said that ... I mean there's a war going on ... the doctors haven't got a cure for cancer – and here's some hillbilly talking about how he doesn't like somebody's clothes...

– And the long hair?...

The thing that most people don't realize is that it's warmer to have long hair. Everybody wants to be warm. Have you ever noticed that Abraham Lincoln had long hair?"

During these years, the music world had two souls – Bob Dylan and Joan Baez on the one hand; on the other the idols of the „more, more, more" culture, many of whom died at a very young age – in 1970 both Janis Joplin of an overdose aged 27 and Jimi Hendrix aged 28 after a night of excess; Jim Morrison of an overdose in 1971.

Today, if I were to create a new version of Edgar Lee Masters' Spoon River Anthology, I would sing the words: „Where are Stephen, Mario and Morning Star, the poet boy, the leader of the Berkeley revolt, the LSD girl? Are they all, all sleeping on some hill?"

Maybe the dream vanished with the death of Robert Kennedy, the white friend of the blacks, who declared to young protesters in Berkeley in November 1966: „Protest should not be allowed, it should be compulsory." Perhaps the dream broke with the death of Martin Luther King, who said: „Non-violence is the answer to all the major political and moral problems of our time; people's need to get the better of oppression and violence without using oppression and violence. People have to find a solution to every human conflict, without resorting to revenge, aggression or reprisals. At the heart of the solution is love. And more – the welfare of the human race lies in the hands of creative, unconventional people."

Maybe the dream is simply slumbering at the bottom of the sea somewhere, just waiting for a new, powerful storm of music to bring it back to life again.

Lello Piazza

Der unsterbliche Traum

Das angesehene amerikanische Wochenblatt „Time" schreibt in seiner Ausgabe vom 24. Dezember 1965: „Aus den Statistiken des FBI geht hervor, dass Jugendliche unter fünfundzwanzig Jahren für 73,4 Prozent der Straftaten wie Mord, Vergewaltigung, Raub und andere schwer wiegende Straftaten verantwortlich sind; sie verursachen 31 Prozent aller Unfälle mit Todesfolge. Die Jugendlichen organisieren Demonstrationen für die Feinde unseres Landes. Sie marschieren mit Plakaten, auf denen anstößige oder beleidigende Parolen stehen... Und die neueste solcher Aktivitäten scheint die Gründung von ‚freien Universitäten' zu sein, an denen sie sich, wie sie sagen, treffen, um das studieren zu können, was an den herkömmlichen Hochschulen nicht unterrichtet wird; Lehrstoffe wie zum Beispiel ‚Die wahre sexuelle Erfahrung' und ‚Die Offenbarungen der Halluzinogene'. Die jungen Männer sehen aus wie Mädchen, die Mädchen wie Männer, ihre Lieder sind endlose Proteste gegen furchtbare Dinge, die ihrer Meinung nach in dieser Gesellschaft geschehen, eine Gesellschaft, die für sie jährlich zwölf Milliarden Dollar für Autos, Gitarren, Anti-Akne-Lotionen, Haarshampoo und immer extravagantere Kleidungsstücke ausgibt."

Dies ist die Stimme des fundamentalistischen Amerikas der sechziger Jahre, das zwei Jahre zuvor in Dallas Augenzeuge wurde, wie Präsident John Kennedy einem Hinterhalt zum Opfer fiel, und drei Jahre später miterleben wird, wie der Friedensnobelpreisträger von 1964, Martin Luther King, und Robert Kennedy, Johns Bruder, der sonst sicher während der Novemberwahlen anstelle des republikanischen Kandidaten Richard Nixon zum Präsidenten gewählt worden wäre, ermordet werden.

Einige Monate vor Erscheinen des „Time"-Artikels wird Lyndon Johnson, Kennedys Vize, als Präsident des Landes in seinem Amt bestätigt. Kaum gewählt, beginnt Johnson unter dem Vorwand von Flottenzwischenfällen im Golf von Tongking mit den Luftangriffen auf Nordvietnam. In den Vereinigten Staaten macht der Ausspruch die Runde: Wir haben für Johnson gestimmt und Goldwater im Weißen Haus vorgefunden (Goldwater war Johnsons Wahlkampfgegner, ein Mann der extremen Rechten, die die Rassentrennung befürwortete).

Vor diesem sozialen und politischen Hintergrund entsteht der Traum der Woodstock-Generation.

Elliott Landy, der die Fotos für diesen Band gemacht hat, erzählte mir Folgendes: „Die Welt schien so dumm zu sein ... Ich dachte, es genügt, die Welt zu fotografieren und den Menschen zu zeigen, wie dumm sie ist (oder wie schön und kreativ sie sein könnte), um die Leute zu ändern. Aus idiotischen Gründen und falschen patriotischen Gefühlen hatten sich die Vereinigten Staaten in den Tunnel eines furchtbaren Krieges in Vietnam verrannt. Also kehrte ich Ende 1967 aus Dänemark (wo ich als Szenenfotograf beim Drehen eines Filmes arbeitete) mit dem erklärten Ziel in die USA zurück, an der Beendigung des Vietnamkrieges mitzuwirken, indem ich die großen Friedenskundgebungen von Washington und New York dokumentierte."

Der Vietnamkrieg gehörte zu den ersten degenerierten Kriegen im letzten Abschnitt unseres Jahrhunderts. Am 16. September 1966 schrieb Arturo Jemolo in der „Stampa" zu diesem Thema: „In den Kriegen des Altertums plünderten die Soldaten die Städte, töteten die Zivilisten und vergewaltigten. Aber das waren Söldner, ein von guten Christen nicht gewählter Beruf. Und Plündern und Vergewaltigen war nicht Pflicht. In den letzten Kriegen unserer Zeit dagegen lautete der Befehl für die Soldaten, auch Handelsschiffe zu versenken, ohne dass die Besatzung sich hätte retten können, vom Flugzeug aus auf die Bevölkerung zu schießen und Flammenwerfer auf bewohnte Häuser zu richten. Der Bombenkrieg gegen Städte ist zu einer normalen Kriegshandlung geworden." Es werden die Fotografien von Larry Barrows, Nick Ut und Dan McCullin sein, die Amerika mit dieser Art von Gräueltaten bekannt machen werden.

Elliott Landy will kein Kriegsfotograf in Vietnam sein: „Ich wollte nicht damit enden, dass ich von einer Bombe getötet oder verstümmelt werde", sagt er.

Zu jener Zeit beginnen seine Erfahrungen mit der Musikwelt.

„Hätte ich diese Musik nicht geliebt, hätte ich sie nicht fotografieren können. Die Faszination der Musiker jener Jahre bestand hauptsächlich in ihrer ganz eigenen Art, Musik zu machen, zu der sie die verborgensten, tiefsten, intimsten und poetischsten Winkel ihrer Seele inspirierten. Die Konzertgestaltung, die sie entwickelten, war völlig neu: Sie beschränkten sich nicht allein auf die Darbietung, sondern kommunizierten mit Jungen und Mädchen im Publikum, luden sie zum Tanzen ein, forderten sie auf, ihren Lebensstil zu ändern und Teil einer großen Friedens- und Liebesgemeinschaft zu werden.

1968 war ich bei den großen psychedelischen Konzerten im Anderson Theater im New Yorker Village und im Fillmore East mit Jimi Hendrix, Jim Morrison, Chuck Berry, außerdem beim Newport Folk Festival mit Joan Baez, Pete Seeger, Janis Joplin und auch in Woodstock. Das veränderte mein Leben und meine Art zu fotografieren grundlegend. Das Fotografieren der Sänger wurde für mich zu einer Verpflichtung, als wäre ich ein Opfer der Ekstase."

Elliott Landy, offiziell zugelassener Fotograf von Woodstock und einer der wenigen Fotografen, denen es gestattet war, während der legendären Konzerte auf der Bühne mit dabei zu sein, hat in dieser denkwürdigen Ära außerordentliche Bilder gemacht und gilt deshalb als einer ihrer „glaubwürdigen" Zeugen. Zum Thema Woodstock-Generation hat er für „Life", „Newsweek" und „Rolling Stone" Titelblätter entworfen. Er war der Autor des Schallplattencovers von *Nashville Skyline* von Bob Dylan und der Alben von „The Band". Einige seiner Fotos sind absolut unvergesslich: Etwa das von Jim Morrison, auf dem er wie ein von Piero della Francesca gemalter Engel wirkt; oder das Foto von Janis Joplin bei ihrem Auftritt im Anderson Theater (ihr Gesicht erinnert an die aus dem irdischen Paradies vertriebene Eva aus dem Fresko von Masaccio). Erinnert sei auch an die Bühnenaufnahmen, die während der Konzerte mit Infrarotfilmen gemacht wurden – wahrhaft beunruhigende Gemälde wie von Basquiat –, oder schließlich jene friedvollen Aufnahmen von Bob Dylan in seiner Wohnung in Woodstock.

Die Jugendlichen waren die Ko-Akteure jener Epoche und bewegten sich wie die Wellen des Meeres im Sturm der Musik. Diese Jugendlichen, die Edgar Friedenberg, Soziologieprofessor in Berkeley, als die wahren Erben des amerikanischen Puritanismus bezeichnete, hatten einen Traum: Sie wollten die Welt verändern, in der sie aufgewachsen waren, indem sie sich dem Krieg widersetzten, indem sie dafür kämpften, dass die amerikanischen Schwarzen einen gerechten Anteil an den bürgerlichen Rechten erhalten, und indem sie die „demokratische Unfreiheit der fortgeschrittenen industriellen Zivilisation" (wie von Marcuse definiert) ablehnten.

„Für diese Schlacht der Ideale wählten sie Musiker zu ihren Anführern", um nochmals Landy zu zitieren. „Aber sie begingen, wie ich meine, einen Fehler. Diese Künstler konnten die Jugendlichen in der Tat mitreißen und bei ihnen eine revolutionäre kulturelle Erfahrung bewirken, die sie aus dem Nebel der Angst führte. Aber als Menschen hatten dieselben Künstler im Allgemeinen tragische und selbstzerstörerische Erfahrungen gemacht. Dylan selbst sagte mir ganz klar, dass er kein Anführer sein will, sondern ganz einfach ein poetisches Gefühl vermitteln möchte."

In diesem Zusammenhang erinnert Furio Colombo an das berühmte Interview, das Dylan

1966 dem „Playboy" gegeben hat, aus dem ich einige Passagen zitiere:

„Warum haben Sie aufgehört, Protestlieder zu komponieren und zu singen?"

„Ich habe mit jedweder Sache aufgehört, die einen Anlass hätte, geschrieben, oder ein Motiv, gesungen zu werden. ‚Protest' ist nicht mein Wort. Ich glaube, das Wort ‚Protest' wurde für Leute erfunden, die dabei sind, sich einer Operation zu unterziehen. … Jedenfalls sind Lieder mit Botschaft, wie jeder weiß, Mist. Nur einsame Mädchen unter vierzehn können vielleicht Zeit dafür haben."

Und etwas später:

„In ihrer Bewunderung ahmen viele junge Leute Ihren Kleidungsstil nach, den ein erwachsener Kommentator ‚verschroben und zweifelsohne schlampig' genannt hat."

„Ich kenne den Typen, der das gesagt hat. … Ich meine, es ist Krieg. … Die Ärzte haben kein Heilmittel gegen Krebs – und da kommt so ein Hinterwäldler und erzählt, daß er meine Kleidung nicht mag."

„Und die langen Haare?"

„Die meisten Leute sind sich nicht darüber im Klaren, dass es wärmer ist, wenn man die Haare lang trägt. Jeder möchte es warm haben. Ist es Ihnen nie aufgefallen, daß Abraham Lincoln lange Haare hatte?"

Die Welt der Musik jener Jahre hatte zwei Seelen: einerseits Bob Dylan und Joan Baez, andererseits die Idole einer Kultur des „more, more, more", von denen einige sehr jung starben: 1970 im Alter von 27 Jahren Janis Joplin an einer Überdosis, mit 28 Jahren Jimi Hendrix nach einer ausschweifenden Nacht, und 1971 Jim Morrison, ebenfalls an einer Überdosis.

Heute, wenn ich Edgar Lee Masters in einer neuen virtuellen *Spoon River Anthologie* imitiere, möchte ich singen: Wo sind Stephen, Mario und Morning Star, der Junge der Poesie, der Anführer der Revolte von Berkeley, das LSD-Mädchen? Schlafen alle, alle, alle auf irgendeinem Hügel?

Vielleicht ist der Traum mit dem Tod von Robert Kennedy zerronnen, mit dem weißen Freund der Schwarzen, mit dem Verschwinden dessen, der im November 1966 in Berkeley den jungen revoltierenden Menschen erklärte: „Widerspruch dürfen wir nicht nur dulden, wir müssen ihn fordern." Vielleicht zerriss der Traum mit dem Tod von Martin Luther King, der behauptete: „Gewaltlosigkeit ist die Antwort auf die entscheidenden politischen und moralischen Probleme unserer Zeit; die Notwendigkeit für den Menschen, über Unterdrückung und Gewalt die Oberhand zu gewinnen, ohne jedoch Unterdrückung und Gewalt anzuwenden. Für jeden menschlichen Konflikt muss der Mensch eine Methode entwickeln, die Rache, Aggressionen und Repressalien ablehnt. Das Fundament einer solchen Methode ist die Liebe. Und weiter: Das Heil des Menschen liegt in den Händen der kreativen Nichtangepassten."

Vielleicht schlummert der Traum nur irgendwo auf dem Grund des Meeres, bereit, von einem neuen mächtigen Sturm der Musik wieder aufgeweckt zu werden.

Lello Piazza

The Pictures / Die Bilder

22-23 Along the march route, peace demonstration at the Pentagon, Washington, 1967 / Entlang der Marschroute, Friedenskundgebung am Pentagon, Washington, 1967
24 Allen Ginsberg supports conscientious objectors, New York, 1967 / Allen Ginsberg unterstützt die Kriegs- dienstverweigerer, die sich der Einberufung aus Gewissensgründen widersetzen, New York, 1967
25 Norman Mailer supports conscientious objectors; my signature is at the top, New York, 1967 / Norman Mailer unterstützt die Kriegsdienstverweigerer aus Gewissensgründen; meine Unterschrift ist die erste von oben, New York, 1967
26 A father helps his son to burn his draft orders as a sign of protest, New York, 1967 / Ein Vater unterstützt seinen Sohn, dessen Einberufungsbefehl als Zeichen seines Protestes zu verbrennen, New York, 1967
27 Norman Mailer at a meeting to support conscientious objectors, New York, 1967 / Norman Mailer bei einer Versammlung zur Unterstützung der Kriegsdienstverweigerer, New York, 1967
28 Reverend William Sloan Coffen appeals to the people to „disobey draft orders", New York, 1967 / Reve- rend William Sloan Coffen ruft die Menschen dazu auf, „sich den Einberufungsbefehlen zu widersetzen", New York, 1967
29 On the run from tear gas at the peace demonstration in front of the Pentagon, Washington, 1967 / Auf der Flucht vor dem Tränengas während der Friedensdemonstration vor dem Pentagon, Washington, 1967
30 A government official photographs the peace demonstration, Pentagon, Washington, 1967 / Ein Regierungsbeamter fotografiert die Friedensdemonstranten am Pentagon, Washington, 1967
31 A demonstrator, possibly a government official, holding a provocative banner at the Pentagon, Washington, 1967 / Ein Demonstrant, vielleicht ein Regierungsbeamter, hält am Pentagon ein provozierendes Plakat hoch, Washington, 1967
32 Along the march route, peace demonstration at the Pentagon, Washington, 1967 / Entlang der Marsch- route, Friedenskundgebung am Pentagon, Washington, 1967
33 Near the Washington Memorial, peace demonstration at the Pentagon, Washington, 1967 / In der Nähe des Washington-Denkmals, Friedenskundgebung am Pentagon, Washington, 1967
34-35 A demonstrator speaking up for war; peace demonstration at the Pentagon, Washington, 1967 / Kriegsbefürworter; Friedenskundgebung am Pentagon, Washington, 1967
36-37 Lincoln Memorial, peace demonstration at the Pentagon, Washington, 1967 / Lincoln Memorial, Friedenskundgebung am Pentagon, Washington, 1967
38 Peace demonstration at the Pentagon, Washington, 1967 / Friedenskundgebung am Pentagon, Washington, 1967
39 Peace demonstration at the Pentagon, Washington, 1967 / Friedenskundgebung am Pentagon, Washington, 1967
40 Peace demonstration in New York, 1968 / Friedenskundgebung in New York, 1968
41 Leonard Bernstein and Barbra Streisand at the Lincoln Center in New York, 1968 / Leonard Bernstein und Barbra Streisand im Lincoln Center in New York, 1968
42 The singer Pearl Bailey at the International Film Awards, New York, 1968 / Die Sängerin Pearl Bailey während der Verleihungsfeier des International Film Awards, New York, 1968
43 Hermione Gingold at the International Film Awards, New York, 1968 / Hermione Gingold während der Verleihungsfeier des International Film Awards, New York, 1968
44 Elizabeth Taylor at the opening night of the film *Dr. Faustus*, which marks Richard Burton's debut as director, New York, 1968 / Elizabeth Taylor bei der Premiere des Films *Dr. Faustus*, Erstregie von Richard Burton, New York, 1968
45 Waiting for Elizabeth Taylor and Richard Burton at the opening night of the film *Dr. Faustus*, New York, 1968 / Warten auf Elizabeth Taylor und Richard Burton bei der Premiere des Films *Dr. Faustus*, New York, 1968
46 Applause at the party to celebrate the publication of Andy Warhol's book, Random House, New York, 1968 / Ein Hurra auf der Party zur Veröffentlichung des Buches von Andy Warhol, Random House, New York, 1968
47 Bobby Darin and Bobby Gentry at a film opening night, New York, 1968 / Bobby Darin und Bobby Gentry bei einer Filmpremiere, New York, 1968
48 The film producer Sam Spiegel at the International Film Awards, New York, 1968 / Der Filmproduzent Sam Spiegel bei der Verleihungsfeier des International Film Awards, New York, 1968
49 The singer Pearl Bailey at the International Film Awards, New York, 1968 / Die Sängerin Pearl Bailey während der Verleihungsfeier des International Film Awards, New York, 1968

50 Arlene Dahl at an opening night celebration, New York, 1968 / Arlene Dahl auf einer Premierenparty, New York, 1968
51 Keir Dullea, Dyan Cannon and Dustin Hoffman at an award ceremony, New York, 1968 / Keir Dullea, Dyan Cannon und Dustin Hoffman bei einer Preisverleihung, New York, 1968
52 Melina Mercouri at an opening night, New York, 1968 / Melina Mercouri während einer Premiere, New York, 1968
53 Richard Harris at the opening night of the film *Camelot*, in which he played the leading role, New York, 1968 / Richard Harris bei der Premiere des Films *Camelot*, dessen Hauptdarsteller er war, New York, 1968
55 Lauren Bacall with Dirk Bogarde at an award ceremony; he is whispering to her: "Smile for the camera!", New York, 1968 / Lauren Bacall mit Dirk Bogarde, der ihr während einer Preisverleihungszeremonie zuflüstert: „Ein Lächeln für die Kamera!", New York, 1968
56 A demonstrator for the right to abortion, New York, 1968 / Ein Demonstrant für das Recht auf Abtreibung, New York, 1968
57 Late for an opening night – the red carpet is being rolled up again, New York, 1968 / Verspätetes Eintreffen zu einer Premiere, als der rote Teppich schon wieder eingerollt wird, New York, 1968
58 Meeting to call for an end to the Vietnam war, Central Park, New York, 1968 / Versammlung für die Beendigung des Vietnamkrieges, Central Park, New York, 1968
59 Demonstrators supporting the war, Bryant Park, New York, 1968 / Kriegsbefürworter, Bryant Park, New York, 1968
60-61 On the run from the police at a peace demonstration in New York, 1968 / Auf der Flucht vor der Polizei während einer Friedenskundgebung, New York, 1968
63 A peace demonstrator, Central Park West, New York, 1968 / Ein Friedensdemonstrant, Central Park West, New York, 1968
64 Protest against industrial diamond mining in South Africa, New York, 1968 / Kundgebung gegen die Diamanten-Bergbau-Industrie in Südafrika, New York, 1968
65 The film producer Darryl F. Zanuck at the International Film Awards, New York, 1968 / Der Filmproduzent Darryl F. Zanuck während der Verleihungsfeier des International Film Awards, New York, 1968
66 Peace demonstrators, Washington Square Park, New York, 1968 / Friedensdemonstranten, Washington Square Park, New York, 1968
67 Lauren Bacall at the International Film Awards, New York, 1968 / Lauren Bacall während der Verleihungs-feier des International Film Awards, New York, 1968
68 Police officers in civilian clothes attack peace demonstrators, Washington Square Park, New York, 1968 / Polizisten in Zivil schlagen auf Friedensdemonstranten ein, Washington Square Park, New York, 1968
69 The police pursue and strike a handicapped civilian, New York, 1968 / Die Polizei verfolgt und schlägt einen Behinderten, New York, 1968
70 Demonstrators supporting the war, Bryant Park, New York, 1968 / Kriegsbefürworter, Bryant Park, New York, 1968
71 Robert Kennedy Jr. Rockefeller Center, New York, 1968 / Robert Kennedy Jr. Rockefeller Center, New York, 1968
72 Crowd at a rock concert, Fillmore East, New York, 1969 / Das Publikum bei einem Rockkonzert, Fillmore East, New York, 1969
73 Crowd at a rock concert in the Anderson Theater, New York, 1968 / Das Publikum bei einem Rockkonzert im Anderson Theater, New York, 1968
74 Marlene Dietrich at a party to celebrate the opening night of her recital, New York, 1968 / Marlene Dietrich auf einer Party zur Premiere ihres Recitals, New York, 1968
75 Marlene Dietrich hides from photographers, New York, 1968 / Marlene Dietrich versteckt sich vor den Fotografen, New York, 1968
76 Demonstration for the right to abortion in front of St. Patrick's Cathedral, New York, 1968 / Demonstration für das Recht auf Abtreibung vor der St. Patrick-Kathedrale, New York, 1968
77 „Hypocrisy – society's message"; demonstration for the right to abortion, New York, 1968 / „Hypocrisy – society's message"; Demonstration für das Recht auf Abtreibung, New York, 1968
78 Britt Eklund at a party, New York, 1968 / Britt Eklund auf einer Party, New York, 1968
79 Faye Dunaway at an opening night, New York, 1968 / Faye Dunaway während einer Premiere, New York, 1968
80 News of the demonstration, Times Square, New York, 1968 / Nachrichten live von der Kundgebung, Times Square, New York, 1968
81 Tiger Morse at the party to celebrate the publication of Andy Warhol's book, Random House, New York, 1968 / Tiger Morse auf der Party zur Veröffentlichung des Buches von Andy Warhol, Random House, New York, 1968
82 Elizabeth Taylor and Richard Burton at the opening night of the film *Dr. Faustus*, New York, 1968 / Elizabeth Taylor und Richard Burton bei der Premiere des Films *Dr. Faustus*, New York, 1968

83 The police arresting a demonstrator who puts on a helmet during a peace march, New York, 1968 / Die Polizei ergreift einen Demonstranten, der während einer Friedensdemonstration einen Schutzhelm trägt, New York, 1968

84 A smile at an opening night, New York, 1968 / Ein Lächeln auf einer Premiere, New York, 1968

85 Joan Collins at a party, New York, 1968 / Joan Collins auf einer Party, New York, 1968

86-87 „A Matter of Innocence", Demonstration for the right to abortion, New York, 1968 / „A Matter of Innocence", Demonstration für das Recht auf Abtreibung, New York, 1968

89 Albert King at the Fillmore East, New York, 1968 / Albert King im Fillmore East, New York, 1968

90-91 B.B. King at the Fillmore East, New York, 1968 / B.B. King im Fillmore East, New York, 1968

92 Buddy Guy at the Newport Folk Festival, Newport, Rhode Island, 1968 / Buddy Guy auf dem Newport Folk Festival, Newport, Rhode Island, 1968

93 Buddy Guy at the Newport Folk Festival, Newport, Rhode Island, 1968 / Buddy Guy auf dem Newport Folk Festival, Newport, Rhode Island, 1968

94 Richie Havens in front of his apartment in East Village, New York, 1968 / Richie Havens vor seinem Apartment im East Village, New York, 1968

95 Richie Havens at the Fillmore East, New York, 1968 / Richie Havens im Fillmore East, New York, 1968

96 Chuck Berry

97 Musician at the Newport Folk Festival, Newport, Rhode Island, 1968 / Musiker auf dem Newport Folk Festival, Newport, Rhode Island, 1968

99 John Lennon and Paul McCartney at the press conference to announce the launch of „Apple Records", New York, 1968 / John Lennon und Paul McCartney während der Pressekonferenz anlässlich der Gründung von „Apple Records", New York, 1968

100 John Lennon and Paul McCartney at the press conference to announce the launch of „Apple Records", New York, 1968 / John Lennon und Paul McCartney während der Pressekonferenz anlässlich der Gründung von „Apple Records", New York, 1968

101 John Lennon and Paul McCartney at the press conference to announce the launch of „Apple Records", New York, 1968 / John Lennon während der Pressekonferenz anlässlich der Gründung von „Apple Records", New York, 1968

102 Roger Daltrey (The Who) gives an interview at the hotel „Room", New York, 1968 / Roger Daltrey (The Who) bei einem Interview im Hotel „Room", New York, 1968

103 Finale of the Who concert at the Anderson Theater, New York, 1968 / Finale des Konzerts der Who im Anderson Theater, New York, 1968

104 Keith Moon (The Who), New York, 1968

105 Keith Moon (The Who) gives an interview at the hotel „Room", New York, 1968 / Keith Moon (The Who) während eines Interviews im Hotel „Room", New York, 1968

106 Elton John, New York, 1969

107 Tom Rush

108 Jefferson Airplane at the Fillmore East, New York, 1968 / Jefferson Airplane im Fillmore East, New York, 1968

109 Procol Harum at the „Joshua Light Show" at the Fillmore East, New York, 1968 / Procol Harum bei der „Joshua Light Show" im Fillmore East, New York, 1968

110-111 The Fugs at the „Anti-Vietnam War Light Show", Anderson Theater, New York, 1968 / The Fugs bei der „Anti-Vietnam War Light Show", Anderson Theater, New York, 1968

112 The Fugs at the „Anti-Vietnam War Light Show", Anderson Theater, New York, 1968 / The Fugs bei der „Anti-Vietnam War Light Show", Anderson Theater, New York, 1968

113 Sly & the Family Stone at the Fillmore East, New York, 1968 / Sly & the Family Stone im Fillmore East, New York, 1968

114-115 John Lee Hooker at the recording studios, New York, 1968 / John Lee Hooker im Aufnahmestudio, New York, 1968

116 Frank Zappa at the Fillmore East, New York, 1968 / Frank Zappa im Fillmore East, New York, 1968

117 Chuck Berry at the Fillmore East, New York, 1968 / Chuck Berry im Fillmore East, New York, 1968

119 Newport Folk Festival, Newport, Rhode Island, 1968

120 Newport Folk Festival, Newport, Rhode Island, 1968

121 Doc Watson at the Newport Folk Festival, Newport, Rhode Island, 1968 / Doc Watson beim Newport Folk Festival, Newport, Rhode Island, 1968

122 Arlo Guthrie and Pete Seeger at the Newport Folk Festival, Newport, Rhode Island, 1968 / Arlo Guthrie und Pete Seeger beim Newport Folk Festival, Newport, Rhode Island, 1968

123 Linda Eastman, Country Joe McDonald, a member of the band and a friend behind the scenes at the Anderson Theater, New York, 1968 / Linda Eastman, Country Joe McDonald, ein Mitglied der Gruppe und eine Freundin hinter den Kulissen des Anderson Theaters, New York, 1968

124 Pete Seeger at the Newport Folk Festival, Newport, Rhode Island, 1968 / Pete Seeger beim Newport Folk Festival, Newport, Rhode Island, 1968

125 Linda Ronstadt at a friend's apartment in East Village, New York, 1968 / Linda Ronstadt in der Wohnung von Freunden im East Village, New York, 1968

126 Tom Paxton and his daughter, 1970 / Tom Paxton und Tochter, 1970

127 The Shaple Singers

128 Joan Baez and Mimi Farina, Newport Folk Festival, Newport, Rhode Island, 1968 / Joan Baez und Mimi Farina, Newport Folk Festival, Newport, Rhode Island, 1968

129 Buffy St. Marie at the Fillmore East, New York, 1968 / Buffy St. Marie im Fillmore East, New York, 1968

130 Buddy Guy at the Newport Folk Festival, Newport, Rhode Island, 1968 / Buddy Guy beim Newport Folk Festival, Newport, Rhode Island, 1968

131 Ramblin' Jack Elliott at the Newport Folk Festival, Newport, Rhode Island, 1968 / Ramblin' Jack Elliott beim Newport Folk Festival, Newport, Rhode Island, 1968

132 Joan Baez at the Newport Folk Festival, Newport, Rhode Island, 1968 / Joan Baez beim Newport Folk Festival, Newport, Rhode Island, 1968

133 Taj Mahal at the Newport Folk Festival, Newport, Rhode Island, 1968 / Taj Mahal beim Newport Folk Festival, Newport, Rhode Island, 1968

134 The group United States of America at the Fillmore East, New York, 1968 / Die Gruppe United States of America im Fillmore East, New York, 1968

135 Eric Clapton (Derek & The Dominoes), Hartford, Connecticut, 1970

136 Melanie at the Bronx, where she grew up, Bronx, New York, 1969 / Melanie in der Bronx, wo sie aufwuchs, Bronx, New York, 1969

137 Eric Clapton (Derek & The Dominoes), Hartford, Connecticut, 1970

139 Jim Morrison (The Doors) at Hunter College, New York, 1968 / Jim Morrison (The Doors) im Hunter College, New York, 1968

140 Jim Morrison (The Doors) at Hunter College, New York, 1968 / Jim Morrison (The Doors) im Hunter College, New York, 1968

141 Jim Morrison (The Doors) at Hunter College, New York, 1968 / Jim Morrison (The Doors) im Hunter College, New York, 1968

142 Jim Morrison (The Doors) at Hunter College, New York, 1968 / Jim Morrison (The Doors) im Hunter College, New York, 1968

143 Robbie Krieger and Jim Morrison (The Doors) after the concert at Hunter College, New York, 1968 / Robbie Krieger und Jim Morrison (The Doors) nach dem Konzert im Hunter College, New York, 1968

144 Jim Morrison (The Doors) at Hunter College, New York, 1968 / Jim Morrison (The Doors) im Hunter College, New York, 1968

145 Jim Morrison (The Doors) at the Fillmore East, New York, 1968 / Jim Morrison (The Doors) im Fillmore East, New York, 1968

146 Melanie at the Bronx, where she grew up, New York, 1969 / Melanie in der Bronx, wo sie aufwuchs, New York, 1969

147 Melanie, Bronx, New York, 1969

148 Melanie, Bronx, New York, 1969

149 Van Morrison and his wife Janet in front of their house, Woodstock, New York, 1969 / Van Morrison und seine Frau Janet vor ihrem Haus, Woodstock, New York, 1969

150 Tim Buckley at the Newport Folk Festival, Newport, Rhode Island, 1968 / Tim Buckley beim Newport Folk Festival, Newport, Rhode Island, 1968

151 Van Morrison, photographed for the album cover *Moondance*, Woodstock, New York, 1969 / Van Morrison, fotografiert für das Cover des Albums *Moondance*, Woodstock, New York, 1969

152 Van Morrison and his wife Janet, Woodstock, New York, 1969 / Van Morrison und seine Frau Janet, Woodstock, New York, 1969

153 Van Morrison holding the album *King Pleasure*, Woodstock, New York, 1969 / Van Morrison hält das Album *King Pleasure* in der Hand, Woodstock, New York, 1969

154-155 Arlo Guthrie at the Newport Folk Festival, Newport, Rhode Island, 1968 / Arlo Guthrie beim Newport Folk Festival, Newport, Rhode Island, 1968

156 Janis Ian at the Newport Folk Festival, Newport, Rhode Island, 1968 / Janis Ian beim Newport Folk Festival, Newport, Rhode Island, 1968

157 Maria Muldau (Jim Kweskin Jug Band) at the Fillmore East, New York, 1968 / Maria Muldau (Jim Kweskin Jug Band) im Fillmore East, New York, 1968

158 Carlos Santana, Nuremberg, Germany, 1975 / Carlos Santana, Nürnberg, Deutschland, 1975

159 Eric Clapton (Derek & The Dominoes), Hartford, Connecticut, 1970

160 Laura Nyro, Long Island, New York, 1970

161 Eric Clapton (Derek & the Dominoes), Hartford, Connecticut, 1970

162 „Kaleidoscope" musician at the Newport Folk Festival, Newport, Rhode Island, 1968 / Musiker vom „Kaleidoscope" beim Newport Folk Festival, Newport, Rhode Island, 1968

163 John Lee Hooker, New York, 1968 (infrared film) / John Lee Hooker, New York, 1968 (Infrarotfilm)
164 John Lee Hooker, New York, 1968 (infrared film) / John Lee Hooker, New York, 1968 (Infrarotfilm)
165 John Lee Hooker, New York, 1968 (infrared film) / John Lee Hooker, New York, 1968 (Infrarotfilm)
166 Ornette Coleman with his son, New York, 1969 (infrared film) / Ornette Coleman mit Sohn, New York, 1969 (Infrarotfilm)
167 Ornette Coleman with his son, Central Park, New York, 1969 (infrared film) / Ornette Coleman mit Sohn, Central Park, New York, 1969 (Infrarotfilm)
168 Albert Ayler at home, Brooklyn, New York, 1969 (infrared film) / Albert Ayler in seinem Haus, Brooklyn, New York, 1969 (Infrarotfilm)
169 Albert Ayler in Prospect Park, Brooklyn, New York, 1969 (infrared film) / Albert Ayler im Prospect Park, Brooklyn, New York, 1969 (Infrarotfilm)
170 Janis Joplin at the Anderson Theater, New York, 1968 / Janis Joplin im Anderson Theater, New York, 1968
171 Janis Joplin at the Fillmore East, New York, 1968 / Janis Joplin im Fillmore East, New York, 1968
172 Janis Joplin at the Anderson Theater, New York, 1968 / Janis Joplin im Anderson Theater, New York, 1968
173 The crowd listens to Janis Joplin and the 'Big Brother's' joint concert at the Newport Folk Festival, Newport, Rhode Island, 1968 / Publikum beim Konzert von Janis Joplin zusammen mit Big Brother während des Newport Folk Festivals in Newport, Rhode Island, 1968
174 Janis Joplin at the „Joshua Light Show", Anderson Theater, New York, 1968 / Janis Joplin bei der „Joshua Light Show", Anderson Theater, New York, 1968
175 Janis Joplin at the „Joshua Light Show", Anderson Theater, New York, 1968 / Janis Joplin bei der „Joshua Light Show", Anderson Theater, New York, 1968
176 Janis Joplin at the „Joshua Light Show", Fillmore East, New York, 1968 / Janis Joplin bei der „Joshua Light Show", Fillmore East, New York, 1968
177 Janis Joplin at the Anderson Theater, New York, 1968 / Janis Joplin im Anderson Theater, New York, 1968
178-179 Janis Joplin, The Big Brother & the Holding Co., party to celebrate the opening of the Fillmore East, New York, 1968 / Janis Joplin, The Big Brother & the Holding Co., Eröffnungsfeier des Fillmore East, New York, 1968
181 Janis Joplin at the Newport Folk Festival, Newport, Rhode Island, 1968 / Janis Joplin beim Newport Folk Festival, Newport, Rhode Island, 1968
182 Janis Joplin and Sam Andrew in Albert Grossmann's office, New York, 1968 / Janis Joplin und Sam Andrew im Büro von Albert Grossmann, New York, 1968
183 Janis Joplin, opening party of the Fillmore East, New York, 1968 / Janis Joplin, Eröffnungsfeier des Fillmore East, New York, 1968
184-185 Janis Joplin and the Big Brother at the Grande Ballroom, Detroit, 1968 / Janis Joplin und The Big Brother im Grande Ballroom, Detroit, 1968
186-187 Ed Sanders and Janis Joplin behind the scene at the Anderson Theater, New York, 1968 / Ed Sanders und Janis Joplin hinter den Kulissen des Anderson Theaters, New York, 1968
188 Janis Joplin and Dave Getz, drummer of the Big Brother, travelling to Detroit, 1968 / Janis Joplin und Dave Getz, Schlagzeuger von Big Brother, auf der Reise nach Detroit, 1968
189 Janis Joplin behind the scenes at the Grande Ballroom, Detroit, 1968 / Janis Joplin hinter den Kulissen des Grande Ballroom, Detroit, 1968
190 Janis Joplin at the premises of the MC5, Detroit, 1968 / Janis Joplin in den Räumlichkeiten der MC5, Detroit, 1968
191 Janis Joplin at New York Airport before a flight to Detroit, 1968 / Janis Joplin am Flughafen von New York vor dem Abflug nach Detroit, 1968
192 Andy Warhol, Janis Joplin and Tim Buckley at „Max's Kansas City" Restaurant, New York, 1968 / Andy Warhol, Janis Joplin und Tim Buckley im Restaurant „Max's Kansas City", New York, 1968
193 Janis Joplin at the Newport Folk Festival, Newport, Rhode Island, 1968 / Janis Joplin beim Newport Folk Festival, Newport, Rhode Island, 1968
194 Andy Warhol and Janis Joplin at „Max's Kansas City" Restaurant, New York, 1968 / Andy Warhol und Janis Joplin im Restaurant „Max's Kansas City", New York, 1968
195 Janis Joplin
196 Janis Joplin and Clive Davis, the President of CBS Records, at a press conference in New York, 1968 / Janis Joplin und Clive Davis, Präsident von CBS Records, auf der Pressekonferenz in New York, 1968
197 Janis Joplin and her Manager Albert Grossmann at the press conference to announce her signing up with CBS Records, New York, 1968 / Janis Joplin und ihr Manager Albert Grossmann auf der Pressekonferenz für den Vertragsabschluss mit CBS Records, New York, 1968
198 Janıs Joplin and Linda Eastman behind the scenes at the Anderson Theater, New York, 1968 / Janis Joplin und Linda Eastman hinter den Kulissen im Anderson Theater, New York, 1968
199 Janis Joplin
200 Janis Joplin

201 Janis Joplin in Albert Grossmann's office, 1968 / Janis Joplin im Büro von Albert Grossmann, 1968
202 Janis leans on Albert Grossmann at the press conference to announce her signing up with CBS Records, New York, 1968 / Auf der Pressekonferenz für den Vertragsabschluss mit CBS Records stützt sich Janis auf Albert Grossmann, New York, 1968
203 Jimi Hendrix at the „Joshua Light Show", Fillmore East, New York, 1968 / Jimi Hendrix bei der „Joshua Light Show" im Fillmore East, New York, 1968
205 Jimi Hendrix at the Fillmore East, New York, 1968 / Jimi Hendrix im Fillmore East, New York, 1968
206-207 The Jimi Hendrix Experience at the „Joshua Light Show", Fillmore East, New York, 1968 / The Jimi Hendrix Experience bei der „Joshua Light Show", Fillmore East, New York, 1968
208 Jimi Hendrix at the Fillmore East, New York, 1968 / Jimi Hendrix im Fillmore East, New York, 1968
209 Jimi Hendrix at the Fillmore East, New York, 1968 / Jimi Hendrix im Fillmore East, New York, 1968
210-211 The Jimi Hendrix Experience at the press conference at the top of the PanAm Building, New York, 1968 / The Jimi Hendrix Experience bei der Pressekonferenz hoch oben im PanAm Building, New York, 1968
212 Jimi Hendrix
213 Jimi Hendrix at the press conference at the top of the PanAm Building, New York, 1968 / Jimi Hendrix während der Pressekonferenz hoch oben im PanAm Building, New York, 1968
214-215 Jimi Hendrix at the press conference held to welcome him back from England, where he had become famous, PanAm Building, New York, 1968 / Jimi Hendrix während der Pressekonferenz, die zu seiner Begrüßung nach seiner Rückkehr aus England gegeben wurde, wo er berühmt geworden ist, PanAm Building, New York, 1968
216 Jimi Hendrix at the press conference at the top of the PanAm Building, New York, 1968 / Jimi Hendrix während der Pressekonferenz hoch oben im PanAm Buildung, New York, 1968
217 Jimi Hendrix at the press conference at the top of the PanAm Building, New York, 1968 / Jimi Hendrix während der Pressekonferenz hoch oben im PanAm Building, New York, 1968
218 Jimi Hendrix at the Fillmore East, New York, 1968 / Jimi Hendrix im Fillmore East, New York, 1968
219 Jimi Hendrix
220 Jimi Hendrix at the press conference at the top of the PanAm Building, New York, 1968 / Jimi Hendrix während der Pressekonferenz hoch oben im PanAm Building, New York, 1968
221 Jimi Hendrix
222 Jimi Hendrix at the press conference at the top of the PanAm Building, New York, 1968 / Jimi Hendrix während der Pressekonferenz hoch oben im PanAm Building, New York, 1968
223 Jimi Hendrix at the press conference at the top of the PanAm Building, New York, 1968 / Jimi Hendrix während der Pressekonferenz hoch oben im PanAm Building, New York, 1968
224 Jimi Hendrix at the Fillmore East, New York, 1968 / Jimi Hendrix im Fillmore East, New York, 1968
225 Jimi Hendrix at the „Joshua Light Show", Fillmore East, New York, 1968 / Jimi Hendrix bei der „Joshua Light Show", Fillmore East, New York, 1968
226 Jimi Hendrix at the Fillmore East, New York, 1968 / Jimi Hendrix im Fillmore East, New York, 1968
227 Jimi Hendrix at the press conference at the top of the PanAm Building, New York, 1968 / Jimi Hendrix während der Pressekonferenz hoch oben im PanAm Building, New York, 1968
228-229 The Band at the „Joshua Light Show", Fillmore East, New York, 1969 / The Band bei der „Joshua Light Show", Fillmore East, New York, 1969
230 Garth Hudson in Woodstock (3 Days of Peace & Music), Bethel, New York, 1969
231 Levon Helm at the Fillmore East, New York, 1969 / Levon Helm im Fillmore East, New York, 1969
232 Richard Manuel (The Band) at the Fillmore Ballroom, San Francisco, 1969 / Richard Manuel (The Band) im Fillmore Ballroom, San Francisco, 1969
233 Levon Helm, Woodstock, New York, 1969
234 Garth Hudson in front of his house overlooking the Ashokan Reserve, Woodstock, 1969 / Garth Hudson vor seinem Haus, von wo aus man das Ashokan-Reservat überblickt, Woodstock, 1969
235 Robbie Robertson, photo session for the album *Music from Big Pink*, Woodstock, New York, 1968 (infrared film) / Robbie Robertson, Fotosession für das Album *Music from Big Pink*, Woodstock, New York, 1968 (Infrarotfilm)
236 Rick Danko, photo session for the album *Music from Big Pink*, Woodstock, New York, 1968 (infrared film) / Rick Danko, Fotosession für das Album *Music from Big Pink*, Woodstock, New York, 1968 (Infrarotfilm)
237 Levon Helm, photo session for the album *Music from Big Pink*, Woodstock, New York, 1968 (infrared film) / Levon Helm, Fotosession für das Album *Music from Big Pink*, Woodstock, New York, 1968 (Infrarotfilm)
238 Rick Danko, photo session for the album *Music from Big Pink*, Woodstock, New York, 1968 (infrared film) / Rick Danko, Fotosession für das Album *Music from Big Pink*, Woodstock, New York, 1968 (Infrarotfilm)
239 Richard Manuel, photo session for the album *Music from Big Pink*, Woodstock, New York, 1968 (infrared film) / Richard Manuel, Fotosession für das Album *Music from Big Pink*, Woodstock, New York, 1968 (Infrarotfilm)
240 The Band; a friend helps to boost morale, Bearsville, Woodstock, New York, 1968 / The Band; eine Freundin hilft, die Moral zu heben, Bearsville, Woodstock, New York, 1968

241 Levon Helm (The Band) in front of his house, Bearsville, Woodstock, New York, 1968 / Levon Helm (The Band) vor seinem Haus, Bearsville, Woodstock, New York, 1968

242 Garth Hudson in front of his house overlooking the Ashokan Reserve, New York, 1969 / Garth Hudson vor seinem Haus, von wo aus man das Ashokan-Reservat überblickt, Woodstock, New York, 1969

243 Richard Manuel (The Band), Woodstock, New York, 1968

244 The Band outside Richard and Garth's house overlooking the Ashokan Reserve, Woodstock, New York, 1969 / The Band im Freien vor dem Haus von Richard und Garth, von wo aus man das Ashokan-Reservat überblickt, Woodstock, New York, 1969

245 Garth Hudson at his house in Spencer Road, overlooking the Ashokan Reserve, Woodstock, New York, 1969 / Garth Hudson im Haus in der Spencer Road, von wo aus man das Ashokan-Reservat überblickt, Woodstock, New York, 1969

246 The Band outside Richard and Garth's house overlooking the Ashokan Reserve, Woodstock, New York, 1969 / The Band im Freien vor dem Haus von Richard und Garth, von wo aus man das Ashokan-Reservat überblickt, Woodstock, New York, 1969

247 Robbie Robertson, Woodstock, New York, 1969

248 The Band at Richard and Garth's house overlooking the Ashokan Reserve, Woodstock, New York, 1969 (infrared film) / The Band im Haus von Richard und Garth, von wo aus man das Ashokan-Reservat überblickt, Woodstock, New York, 1969 (Infrarotfilm)

249 The Band outside Richard and Garth's house overlooking the Ashokan Reserve, Woodstock, New York, 1969 / The Band im Freien vor dem Haus von Richard und Garth, von wo aus man das Ashokan-Reservat überblickt, Woodstock, New York, 1969

250 Rick Danko (The Band), Woodstock, New York, 1968

251 Members of The Band and friends with Rick Danko on the way to the pond, Woodstock, New York, 1968 / Mitglieder der Band und Freunde mit Rick Danko auf dem Weg zum Weiher, Woodstock, New York, 1968

252 Garth Hudson (The Band) at the pond, Woodstock, New York, 1968 / Garth Hudson (The Band) am Weiher, Woodstock, New York, 1968

253 Robbie and Dominique Robertson, Woodstock, New York, 1968 / Robbie und Dominique Robertson, Woodstock, New York, 1968

254 Garth Hudson jokes for the camera, Hollywood Hills, Los Angeles, 1969 / Garth Hudson macht vor der Kamera Scherze, Hollywood Hills, Los Angeles, 1969

255 Levon Helm (The Band) in front of his house, Bearsville, Woodstock, New York, 1968 / Levon Helm (The Band) vor seinem Haus, Bearsville, Woodstock, New York, 1968

256 „Next Of Kin", Relatives and friends of The Band at Rick Danko's brother's farm, Canada, 1968 / „Next Of Kin", Verwandte und Freunde der Band auf der Farm des Bruders von Rick Danko, Kanada, 1968

257 The Band in front of their house, which they jokingly named „Big Pink", Easter Sunday, West Saugerties, New York, 1968 / The Band vor ihrem Haus, das scherzhaft „Big Pink" genannt wird, Ostersonntag, West Saugerties, New York, 1968

258 The Band, taken for the cover of the album *The Band* (Levon is standing with his back to the camera), Woodstock, New York, 1969 / The Band, Fotosession für das Album *The Band* (Levon steht mit dem Rücken zur Kamera), Woodstock, New York, 1969

259 The Band pose with their Hudson in front of „Big Pink", Woodstock, New York, 1969 / The Band posiert mit ihrem Hudson vor „Big Pink", Woodstock, New York, 1969

260 Levon Helm behind the scenes at the Fillmore East, New York, 1969 / Levon Helm hinter den Kulissen des Fillmore East, New York, 1969

261 Robbie and Dominique Robertson – Albert in the mirror – behind the scenes at the Fillmore East, New York, 1969 / Robbie und Dominique Robertson – Albert im Spiegel – hinter den Kulissen des Fillmore East, New York, 1969

262 The Band, photograph for the album *Music From Big Pink*, Bearsville, Woodstock, New York, 1968 / The Band, Foto für das Album *Music From Big Pink*, Bearsville, Woodstock, New York, 1968

263 The Band and friends, including Albert and Sally Grossmann, behind the scenes at the Fillmore East, New York, 1969 / The Band und Freunde, u. a. Albert und Sally Grossmann, hinter den Kulissen des Fillmore East, New York, 1969

264 The Band in front of „Big Pink", Easter Sunday, West Saugerties, New York, 1968 / The Band vor dem „Big Pink", Ostersonntag, West Saugerties, New York, 1968

265 The Band playing ball in front of Levon and Rick's house, Bearsville, Woodstock, New York, 1968 / The Band beim Ballspiel vor dem Haus von Levon und Rick, Bearsville, Woodstock, New York, 1968

266 The Band at Levon and Rick's house, Bearsville, Woodstock, New York, 1968 / The Band im Haus von Levon und Rick, Bearsville, Woodstock, New York, 1968

267 The Band in the kitchen at „Big Pink", Easter Sunday, West Saugerties, New York, 1968 / The Band in der Küche von „Big Pink", Ostersonntag, West Saugerties, New York, 1968

268 Rick Danko with his dog Hamlet, a gift from Dylan, in his house at Zena Road, Woodstock, New York,

1969 / Rick Danko mit seinem Hund Hamlet, einem Geschenk von Dylan, in seinem Haus in der Zena Road, Woodstock, New York, 1969

269 Richard Manuel at his house at Spencer Road, Woodstock, 1969 / Richard Manuel in seinem Haus in der Spencer Road, Woodstock, New York, 1969

270 The Band recording the album *The Band* at Sammy Davis Jr.'s house, Hollywood Hills, Los Angeles, 1968 / The Band während der Aufnahmen des Albums *The Band* im Haus von Sammy Davis Jr. Hollywood Hills, Los Angeles, 1968

271 Robbie Robertson and Levon Helm rehearsing at Rick Danko's house in Zena Road, Woodstock, New York, 1969 / Robbie Robertson und Levon Helm bei der Probe im Haus von Rick Danko in der Zena Road, Woodstock, New York, 1969

272 The Band at the pond behind „Big Pink", West Saugerties, New York, 1968 / The Band am Weiher hinter dem „Big Pink", West Saugerties, New York, 1968

273 Robbie, who has fallen ill before a concert due to be given by The Band, is given hypnosis treatment, San Francisco, 1969 / Robbie, der vor einem Konzert der Band krank wurde, wird hypnotisiert, San Francisco, 1969

274 Robbie Robertson, Albert Grossmann, Bili Graham and John Simon in a lift, San Francisco, 1969 / Robbie Robertson, Albert Grossmann, Bili Graham und John Simon im Lift, San Francisco, 1969

275 Robbie with John Simon, Albert Grossmann, Levon and Rick after the hypnosis at the hotel, San Francisco, 1969 / Robbie mit John Simon, Albert Grossmann, Levon und Rick nach der Hypnose im Hotel, San Francisco, 1969

276 The Band in the basement of Rick Danko's house in Zena Road, Woodstock, New York, 1969 / The Band im Kellergeschoss des Hauses von Rick Danko in der Zena Road, Woodstock, New York, 1969

277 Levon Helm at the Fillmore East, New York, 1969 / Levon Helm im Fillmore East, New York, 1969

278-279 Bob Dylan and The Band, Woody Guthrie Memorial Concert, Carnegie Hall, New York, 1968 / Bob Dylan und The Band, Woody Guthrie Memorial Concert, Carnegie Hall, New York, 1968

280 Elliott Landy at the photo session for the „Saturday Evening Post", photographed by Dylan, Woodstock, New York, 1968 / Elliott Landy während des Fototermins für die „Saturday Evening Post", von Dylan fotografiert, Woodstock, New York, 1968

281 Bob Dylan, „Take one like this", at the house in Ohayo Mountain Road, Woodstock, New York, 1970 / Bob Dylan, „Take one like this", im Haus in der Ohayo Mountain Road, Woodstock, New York, 1970

282 Bob Dylan, „How about this?" at the house in Ohayo Mountain Road, Woodstock, New York, 1970 / Bob Dylan, „How about this?", im Haus in der Ohayo Mountain Road, Woodstock, New York, 1970

283 Bob Dylan at his house in Ohayo Mountain Road, Woodstock, New York, 1970 / Bob Dylan in seinem Haus in der Ohayo Mountain Road, Woodstock, New York, 1970

284 Bob Dylan with his children Jesse, Anna and Maria at his house in Ohayo Mountain Road, Woodstock, New York, 1970 / Bob Dylan mit seinen Kindern Jesse, Anna und Maria in seinem Haus in der Ohayo Mountain Road, Woodstock, New York, 1970

285 Bob Dylan on the trampoline with his daughter Anna at his house in Ohayo Mountain Road, Woodstock, New York, 1970 / Bob Dylan mit seiner Tochter Anna auf dem Trampolin vor seinem Haus in der Ohayo Mountain Road, Woodstock, New York, 1970

286 Bob Dylan photographs Elliott and Jesse at the photo session for the „Saturday Evening Post", Woodstock, New York, 1968 / Bob Dylan fotografiert Elliott und Jesse während des Fototermins für die „Saturday Evening Post", Woodstock, New York, 1968

287 Bob Dylan photographs Elliott and Jesse at the photo session for the „Saturday Evening Post", Woodstock, New York, 1968 / Bob Dylan fotografiert Jesse und Elliott während des Fototermins für die „Saturday Evening Post", Woodstock, New York, 1968

288 Bob and Sara Dylan with their son Jesse at the Byrdcliff house, Woodstock, New York, 1968 / Bob und Sara Dylan mit ihrem Sohn Jesse im Haus in Byrdcliff, Woodstock, New York, 1968

289 Bob Dylan in his living room at the Byrdcliff house, Woodstock, New York, 1968 / Bob Dylan in seinem Wohnzimmer im Haus in Byrdcliff, Woodstock, New York, 1968

290-291 Bob Dylan with his daughter Anna at his house in Ohayo Mountain Road, Woodstock, New York, 1970 / Bob Dylan mit seiner Tochter Anna im Haus in der Ohayo Mountain Road, Woodstock, New York, 1970

292 Bob, Sara, Jesse, Anna and Sam Dylan at home, Byrdcliff, Woodstock, New York, 1968 / Bob, Sara, Jesse, Anna und Sam Dylan zuhause, Byrdcliff, Woodstock, New York, 1968

293 Bob Dylan with his children Sam and Anna at his house in Ohayo Mountain Road, Woodstock, New York, 1970 / Bob Dylan mit seinen Kindern Sam und Anna im Haus in der Ohayo Mountain Road, Woodstock, New York, 1970

294-295 Bob Dylan with his son Jesse at the Byrdcliff house, Woodstock, New York, 1968 / Bob Dylan mit seinem Sohn Jesse im Haus in Byrdcliff, Woodstock, New York, 1968

296 Bob Dylan on his truck in front of the Byrdcliff house, Woodstock, New York, 1968 / Bob Dylan auf seinem Lastwagen vor dem Haus in Byrdcliff, Woodstock, New York, 1968

297 Bob Dylan near my house, photo session for *Nashville Skyline*, Woodstock, New York, 1968 / Bob Dylan in der Nähe meines Hauses, Fotosession für *Nashville Skyline*, Woodstock, New York, 1968

298-299 Levon Helm, Bob Dylan, Rick Danko with Shredni Volper in the „Lone Star"-Café, New York, 1983 /
Levon Helm, Bob Dylan, Rick Danko mit Shredni Volper im „Lone Star"-Café, New York, 1983
300 Bob Dylan with his children Jesse and Maria at the Byrdcliff house, Woodstock, New York, 1968 /
Bob Dylan mit seinen Kindern Jesse und Maria im Haus in Byrdcliff, Woodstock, New York, 1968
301 Bob Dylan with friends in the market square in Woodstock town, New York, 1968 / Bob Dylan mit
Freunden auf dem Marktplatz der Stadt Woodstock, 1968
302 Bob Dylan on his daughter's birthday at his house in Bleecker Street, New York, 1970 / Bob Dylan am
Geburtstag seiner Tochter in seinem Haus in der Bleecker Street, New York, 1970
303 Bob Dylan at his Byrdcliff house, photo session for *Nashville Skyline*, Woodstock, New York, 1968 / Bob
Dylan in seinem Haus in Byrdcliff, Fotosession für *Nashville Skyline*, Woodstock, New York, 1968
304 Bob and Sara Dylan in the summerhouse at their home in Byrdcliff, Woodstock, New York, 1968 /
Bob und Sara Dylan in der Laube des Hauses in Byrdcliff, Woodstock, New York, 1968
305 Bob Dylan at his Byrdcliff house, *Nashville Skyline* album cover, Woodstock, New York, 1968 /
Bob Dylan in seinem Haus in Byrdcliff, Cover des Albums *Nashville Skyline*, Woodstock, New York, 1968
306 Bob Dylan in the summerhouse at his home in Byrdcliff, Woodstock, New York, 1968 / Bob Dylan in der
Laube seines Hauses in Byrdcliff, Woodstock, New York, 1968
307 Bob Dylan in Madison Square Gardens, New York, 1978 / Bob Dylan im Madison Square Garden,
New York, 1978
308-309 (above) Woodstock Festival; photograph taken using a widelux panorama camera, Bethel, New
York, 1969 / (oben) Woodstock Festival; eine mit dem Panoramaapparat Widelux aufgenommene Fotografie,
Bethel, New York, 1969
308-309 (below) The revolving stage, Woodstock Festival, Bethel, New York, 1969 / (unten) Die Bühne, die
so konstruiert ist, dass sie sich drehen kann, Woodstock Festival, Bethel, New York, 1969
310 Janis Joplin in the music pavilion, Woodstock Festival, Bethel, New York, 1969 / Janis Joplin im
Musikerpavillon, Woodstock Festival, Bethel, New York, 1969
311 Joe Cocker, Woodstock (3 Days of Peace & Music), Bethel, New York, 1969
312 Joan Baez (with her back to the camera) on stage, Woodstock (3 Days of Peace & Music), Bethel, New
York, 1969 / Joan Baez (mit dem Rücken zur Kamera) auf der Bühne, Woodstock (3 Days of Peace & Music),
Bethel, New York, 1969
313 Ravi Shankar, Woodstock (3 Days of Peace & Music)
314 Johnny Winter, Woodstock Festival, Bethel, New York, 1969
315 Richie Havens, Woodstock (3 Days of Peace & Music), Bethel, New York, 1969
316 Blood, Sweat & Tears, Woodstock Festival, Bethel, New York, 1969
317 Tim Hardin, Woodstock Festival, Bethel, New York, 1969
318 Ten Years After, Woodstock Festival, Bethel, New York, 1969
319 John Fogerty (Creedence Clearwater Revival), Woodstock Festival, Bethel, New York, 1969
320 Arlo Guthrie, Woodstock (3 Days of Peace & Music), Bethel, New York, 1969
321 Max Yasgur, the owner of the grounds on which the festival was held, Woodstock (3 Days of Peace &
Music), Bethel, New York, 1969 / Max Yasgur, der Besitzer des Geländes, auf dem sich das Woodstock
Festival (3 Days of Peace & Music) abspielte, Bethel, New York, 1969
322-323 Max Yasgur, Woodstock (3 Days of Peace & Music), Bethel, New York, 1969,
324 Woodstock (3 Days of Peace & Music), Bethel, New York, 1969
325 Max Yasgur and Martin Scorsese (below), giving Max the peace sign, Woodstock Festival, Bethel, New
York, 1969 / Max Yasgur und Martin Scorsese (unten), der Max mit dem Friedenszeichen antwortet,
Woodstock Festival, Bethel, New York, 1969
326-327 The sound tower, Woodstock (3 Days of Peace & Music), Bethel, New York, 1969 / Der Soundturm,
Woodstock (3 Days of Peace & Music), Bethel, New York, 1969
329 Richie Havens, Woodstock (3 Days of Peace & Music), Bethel, New York, 1969 / Richie Havens,
Woodstock (3 Days of Peace & Music), Bethel, New York, 1969
330 Leslie Loaf on the side stage, Woodstock (3 Days of Peace & Music), Bethel, New York, 1969 / Leslie
Loaf auf der Seitenbühne, Woodstock (3 Days of Peace & Music), Bethel, New York, 1969
331 Michael Lang, who masterminded the whole Woodstock concept (3 Days of Peace & Music), Bethel, New
York, 1969 / Michael Lang, der Erfinder und geistige Urheber von Woodstock (3 Days of Peace & Music),
Bethel, New York, 1969
332 Richie Havens, Woodstock (3 Days of Peace & Music), Bethel, New York, 1969
333 Swami Satchtananda, Woodstock (3 Days of Peace & Music), Bethel, New York, 1969
334 The sale of a spiritual underground newspaper, Woodstock Festival, Bethel, New York, 1969 / Verkauf
einer spirituellen Underground-Zeitschrift, Woodstock Festival, Bethel, New York, 1969
335 A couple with the festival program, Woodstock (3 Days of Peace & Music), Bethel, New York, 1969 / Ein
Paar mit den Festival-Programmen, Woodstock (3 Days of Peace & Music), Bethel, New York, 1969
336-337 Woodstock (3 Days of Peace & Music), Bethel, New York, 1969

338-339 Woodstock (3 Days of Peace & Music), Bethel, New York, 1969
340 Joe Cocker's band, Woodstock (3 Days of Peace & Music), Bethel, New York, 1969 / Die Band von Joe Cocker, Woodstock (3 Days of Peace & Music), Bethel, New York, 1969
341 Woodstock (3 Days of Peace & Music), Bethel, New York, 1969
342 Joe Cocker, Woodstock (3 Days of Peace & Music), Bethel, New York, 1969
343 Joe Cocker, Woodstock (3 Days of Peace & Music), Bethel, New York, 1969
344 Woodstock (3 Days of Peace & Music), Bethel, New York, 1969
345 Woodstock (3 Days of Peace & Music), Bethel, New York, 1969
346 Woodstock (3 Days of Peace & Music), Bethel, New York, 1969
347 Woodstock (3 Days of Peace & Music), Bethel, New York, 1969
348 Woodstock (3 Days of Peace & Music), Bethel, New York, 1969
349 Woodstock (3 Days of Peace & Music), Bethel, New York, 1969
350 Woodstock (3 Days of Peace & Music), Bethel, New York, 1969
351 Joan Baez, Woodstock Festival, Bethel, New York, 1969
352 Woodstock (3 Days of Peace & Music), Bethel, New York, 1969
353 The stage was rotated, Woodstock Festival, Bethel, New York, 1969 / Die Bühne wurde gedreht, Woodstock Festival, Bethel, New York, 1969
354-355 Woodstock (3 Days of Peace & Music), Bethel, New York, 1969
356 Woodstock (3 Days of Peace & Music), Bethel, New York, 1969
357 Woodstock (3 Days of Peace & Music), Bethel, New York, 1969
358-359 During the storm I took shelter under the tribune, Woodstock Festival, Bethel, New York, 1969 / Während des Gewitters flüchtete ich mich unter die Tribüne, Woodstock Festival, Bethel, New York, 1969
360-361 Woodstock (3 Days of Peace & Music), Bethel, New York, 1969
362-363 In the morning; Swami Satchtananda's fans, Woodstock Festival, Bethel, New York, 1969 / Am Morgen; die Anhänger von Swami Satchtananda, Woodstock Festival, Bethel, New York, 1969
364 Woodstock (3 Days of Peace & Music), Bethel, New York, 1969
365 Woodstock (3 Days of Peace & Music), Bethel, New York, 1969
366 Jerry Garcia, Woodstock Festival, Bethel, New York, 1969
367 Janis Joplin, Woodstock Festival, Bethel, New York, 1969
368 Garth Hudson (The Band), Woodstock Festival, Bethel, New York, 1969
369 Melanie, still one of my favorite singers today, Woodstock Festival, Bethel, New York, 1969 / Melanie, bis heute eine meiner liebsten Sängerinnen, Woodstock Festival, Bethel, New York, 1969
370-371 Ravi Shankar, Woodstock Festival, Bethel, New York, 1969
372-373 Ravi Shankar in the rain, Woodstock Festival, Bethel, New York, 1969 / Ravi Shankar im Regen, Woodstock Festival, Bethel, New York, 1969
374-375 The sound tower, Woodstock (3 Days of Peace & Music), Bethel, New York, 1969 / Der Soundturm, Woodstock (3 Days of Peace & Music), Bethel, New York, 1969
376-377 Woodstock (3 Days of Peace & Music), Bethel, New York, 1969
378 A view of the public tribunes, Woodstock (3 Days of Peace & Music), Bethel, New York, 1969 / Blick auf die für alle freigegebene Bühne, Woodstock (3 Days of Peace & Music), Bethel, New York, 1969
379 The public stage, Woodstock Festival, Bethel, New York, 1969 / Die für alle zugelassene Bühne, Woodstock Festival, Bethel, New York, 1969
380 The Gratetful Dead, Woodstock (3 Days of Peace & Music), Bethel, New York, 1969 / The Grateful Dead, Woodstock (3 Days of Peace & Music), Bethel, New York, 1969
381 Garth Hudson (The Band), Woodstock Festival, Bethel, New York, 1969 / Garth Hudson (The Band), Woodstock Festival, Bethel, New York, 1969
382-383 Before the rain, Woodstock Festival, Bethel, New York, 1969 / Vor dem Regen, Woodstock Festival, Bethel, New York, 1969
384 Woodstock (3 Days of Peace & Music), Bethel, New York, 1969
385 Two navels and a waistcoat, side stage, Woodstock (3 Days of Peace & Music), Bethel, New York, 1969 / Zwei Nabel und eine Weste, Seitenbühne, Woodstock (3 Days of Peace & Music), Bethel, New York, 1969
386 Woodstock (3 Days of Peace & Music), Bethel, New York, 1969
387 Woodstock (3 Days of Peace & Music), Bethel, New York, 1969
388-389 Woodstock (3 Days of Peace & Music), Bethel, New York, 1969
391 Woodstock (3 Days of Peace & Music), Bethel, New York, 1969
396-397 With my family (Leslie, Bo, Joiwind) and our bus in Athens, 1976 / Mit meiner Familie (Leslie, Bo, Joiwind) und unserem Autobus, Athen, 1976

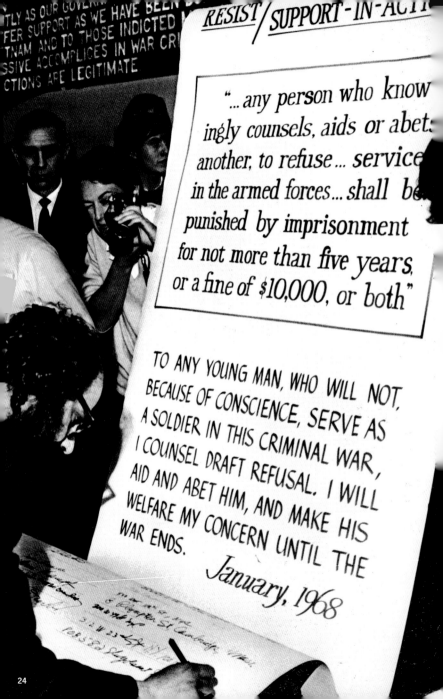

TLY AS OUR GOVERN
FER SUPPORT AS WE HAVE BEEN
TNAM AND TO THOSE INDICTED
SSIVE ACCOMPLICES IN WAR CRI
CTIONS ARE LEGITIMATE.

RESIST / SUPPORT-IN-ACTI

"... any person who know
ingly counsels, aids or abet
another, to refuse... service
in the armed forces... shall be
punished by imprisonment
for not more than five years,
or a fine of $10,000, or both"

TO ANY YOUNG MAN, WHO WILL NOT,
BECAUSE OF CONSCIENCE, SERVE AS
A SOLDIER IN THIS CRIMINAL WAR,
I COUNSEL DRAFT REFUSAL. I WILL
AID AND ABET HIM, AND MAKE HIS
WELFARE MY CONCERN UNTIL THE
WAR ENDS.

January, 1968

WE STAND BESIDE THE MEN WHO HAVE BEEN INDICTED FOR
SUPPORT OF DRAFT RESISTANCE. IF THEY ARE SENTENCED, WE,
TOO, MUST BE SENTENCED. IF THEY ARE IMPRISONED WE WILL
TAKE THEIR PLACES AND WILL CONTINUE TO USE WHAT MEANS
WE CAN TO BRING THIS WAR TO AN END. WE WILL NOT STAND BY

...LENTLY AS OUR GOVERNMENT CONDUCTS A CRIMINAL WAR. WE WILL CONTINUE
...OFFER SUPPORT AS WE HAVE BEEN DOING TO THOSE WHO REFUSE TO SERVE
...VIETNAM AND TO THOSE INDICTE... MEN AND ALL OTHERS WHO REFUSE TO
...PASSIVE ACCOMPLICES IN WAR ...ES. THE WAR IS ILLEGITIMATE AND
...R ACTIONS ARE LEGITIMATE.

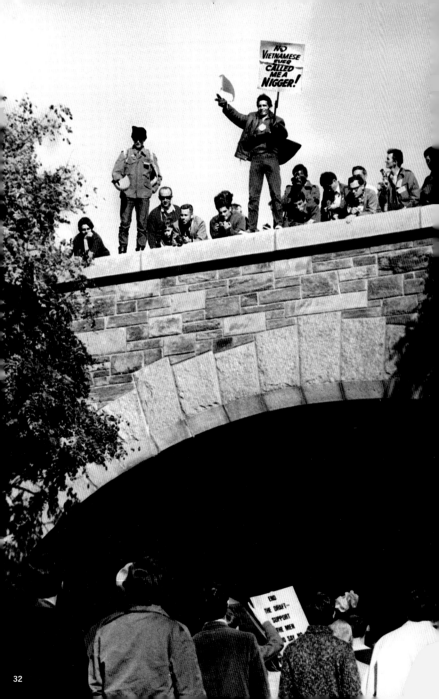

SUPPORT OUR GIs ... BRING THEM H

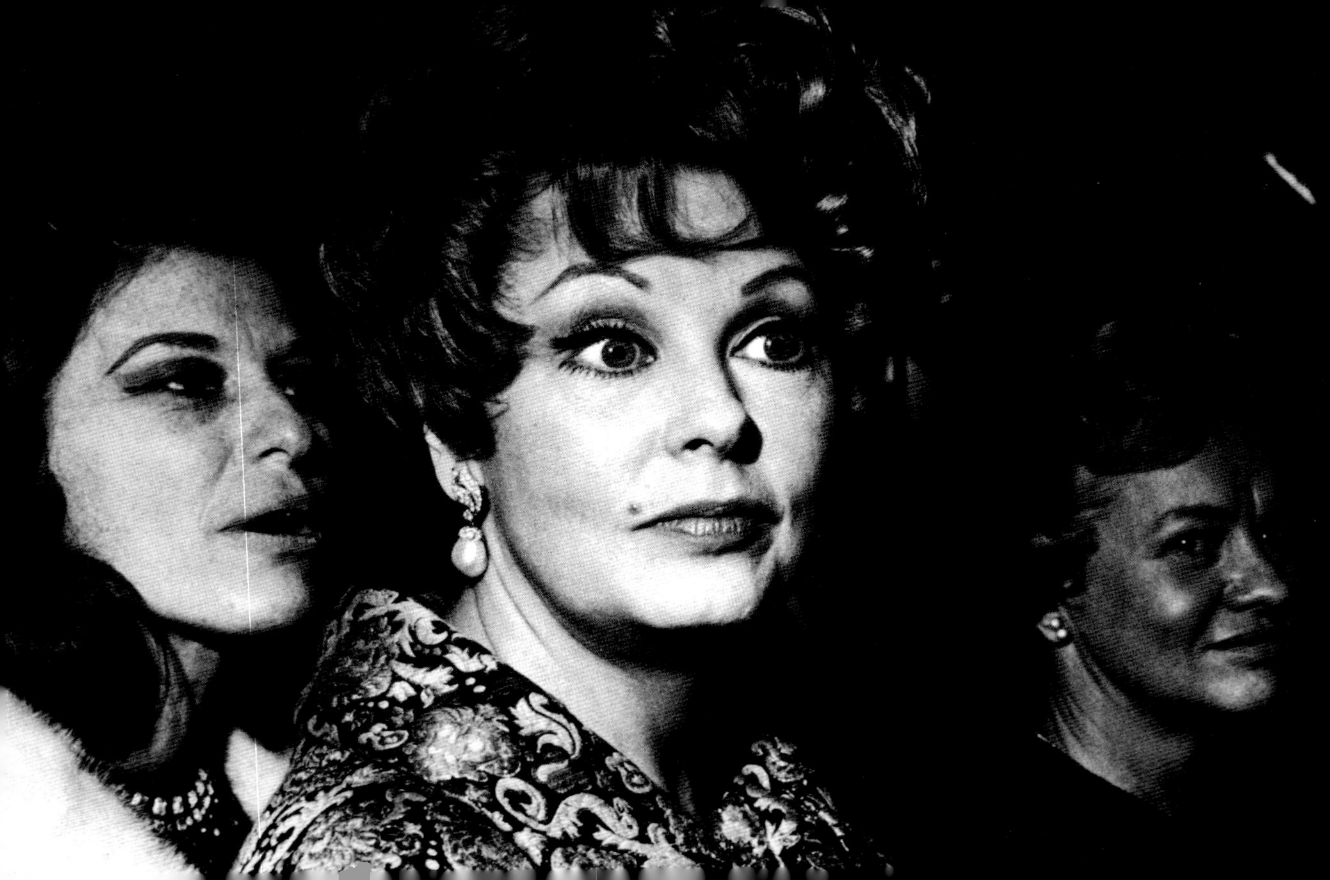

Hollywood Star Gazette

EXTR

BLESSED ARE PEACE & LO
GENERAL WASTE-MORE LA

OR DEMANDS

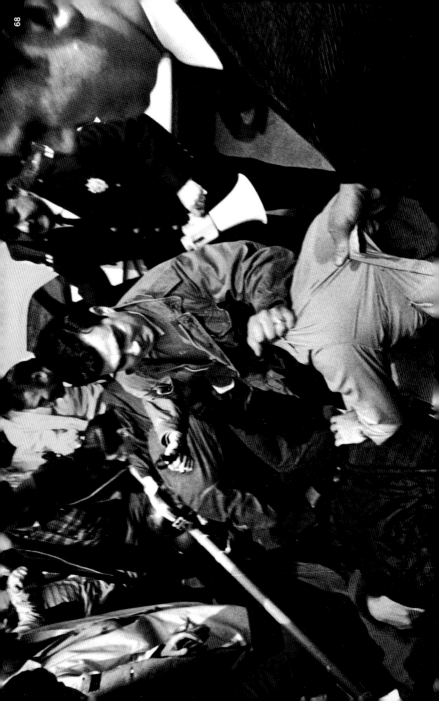

VIVIEN LEIGH
LESLIE HOWARD
OLIVIA de HAVILLAND

A SELZNICK INTERNATIONAL PICTURE · VICTOR FLEMING
METRO GOLDWYN MAYER
STEREOPHONIC SOUND
METROCOLOR

RESERVED SEAT ENGAGEMENT
NOW PLAYING
UA RIVOLI THEATRE

ENTRANCE RIVOLI ON BROADWAY

PREMIERE
ENGAGEMENT
NOW
PLAYING
RIVOLI

In the splendor of Technicolor

"GONE WITH
THE WIND"

RESERVED SEAT
ENGAGEMENT

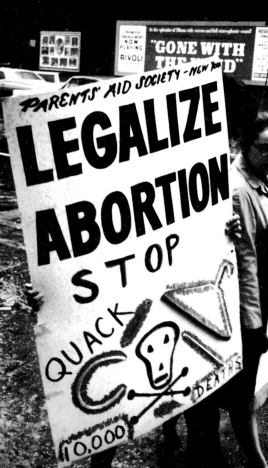

PARENTS' AID SOCIETY — NEW YORK
LEGALIZE
ABORTION
STOP
QUACK
DEATHS
10,000

STOP Killing Mothers

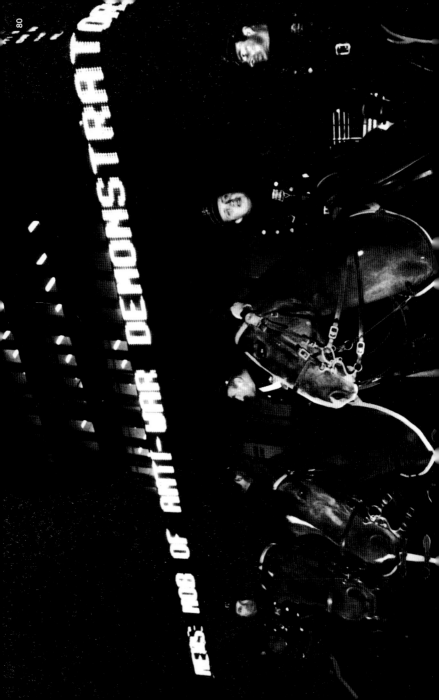

A Matter of Innoce

TECHNICOLOR   A UNIVERSAL

...ADE DELIGHTFULLY FRESH BY A HEAP OF ...

vor Howard
...ashi Kapoor "A Matter of Innocence"

SHE
ISN'T THE
GIRL YOU
THOUGHT
YOU
KNEW!

SELLING
NOW! 70%

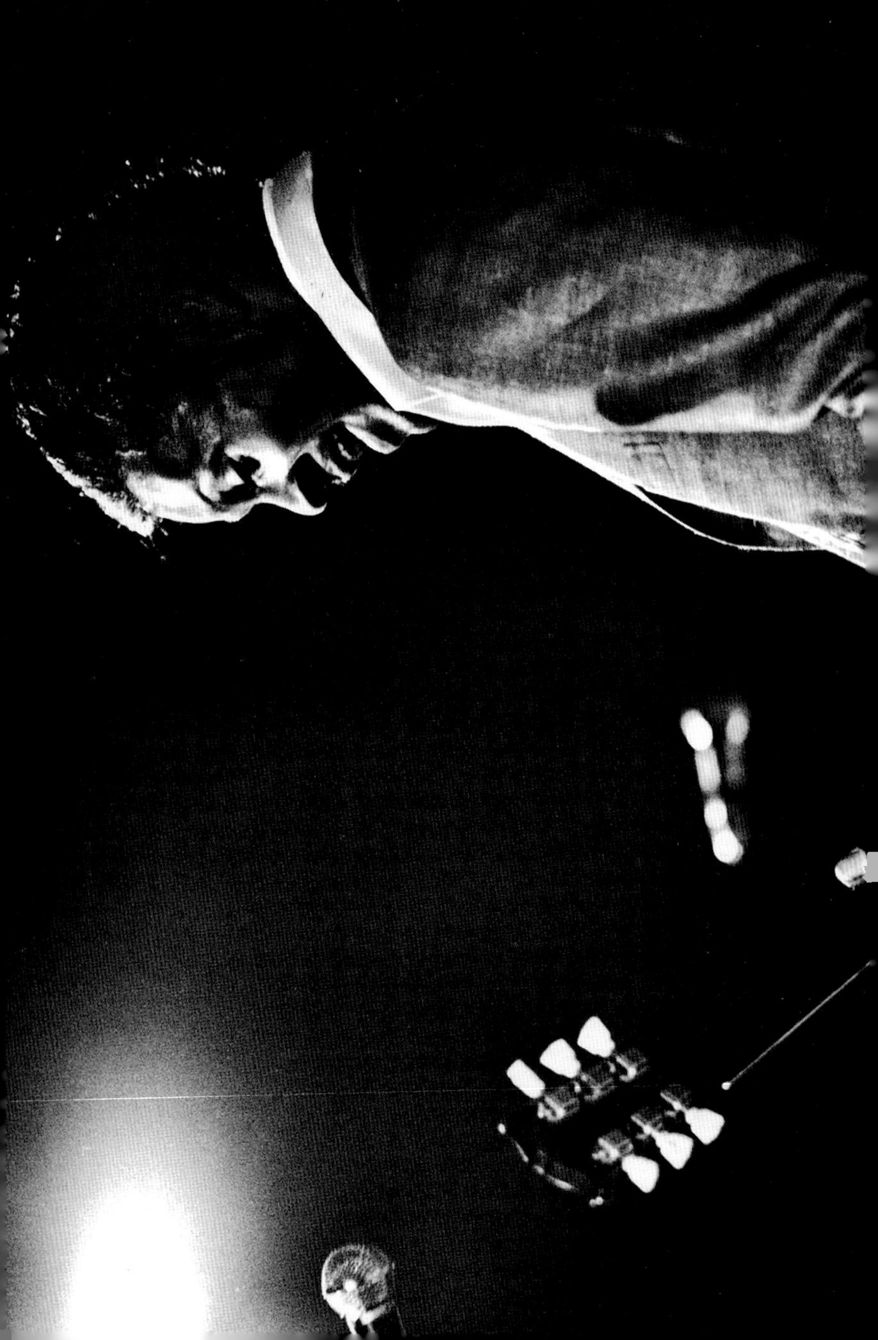

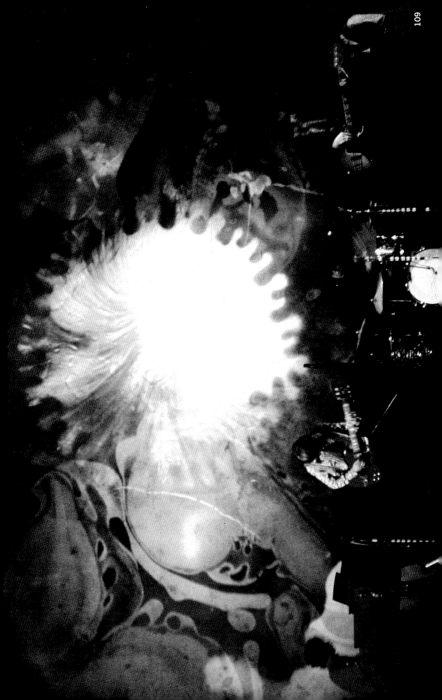

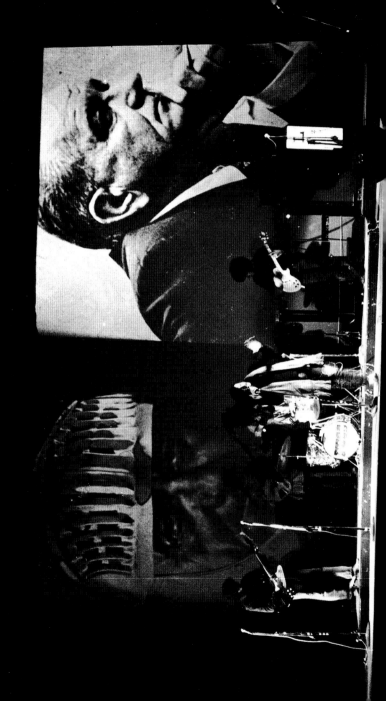

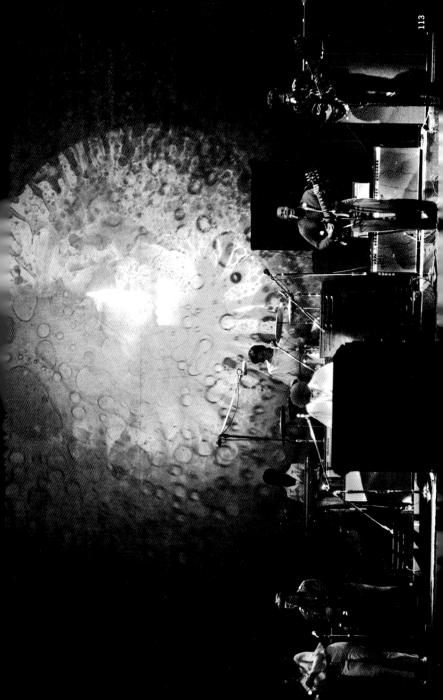

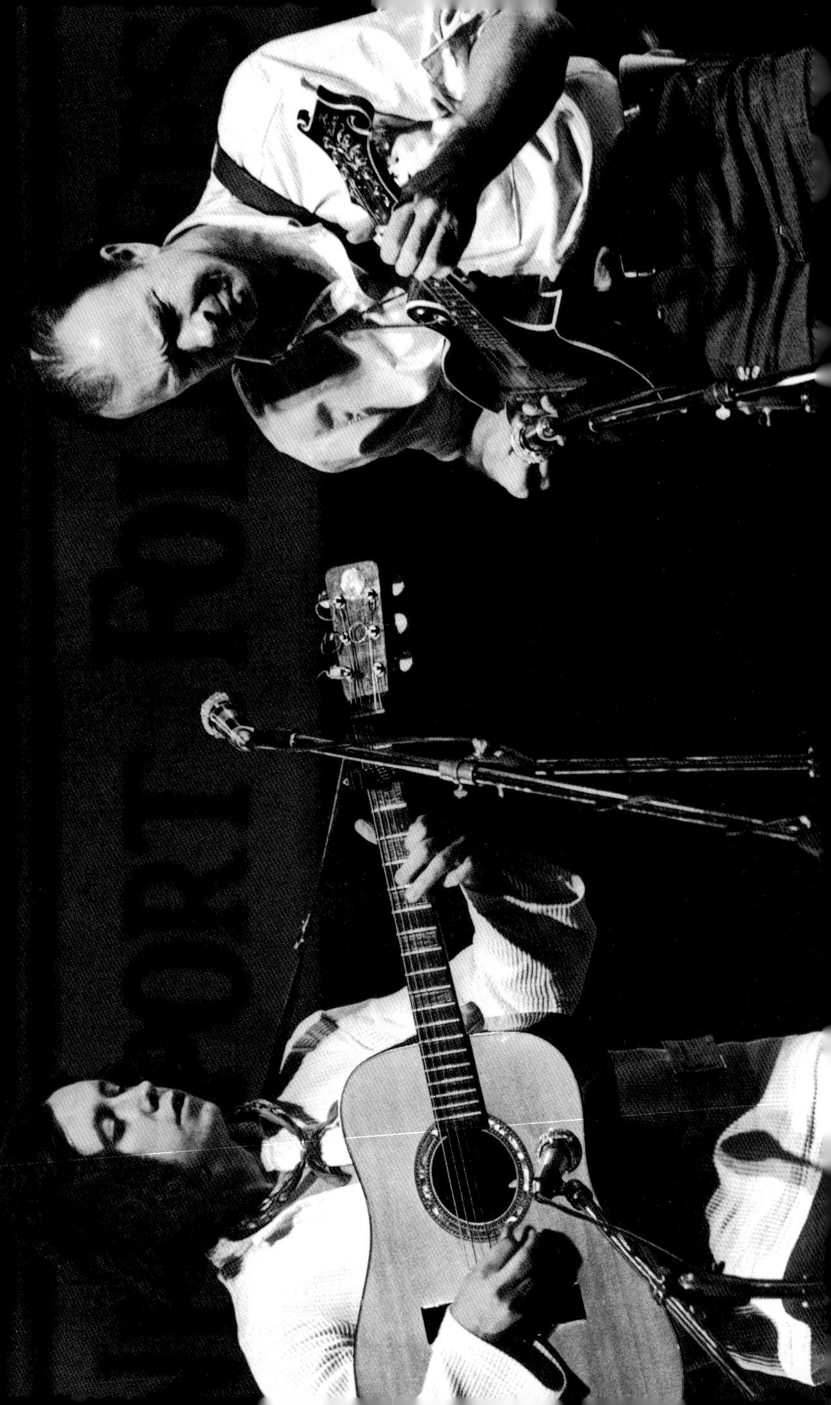

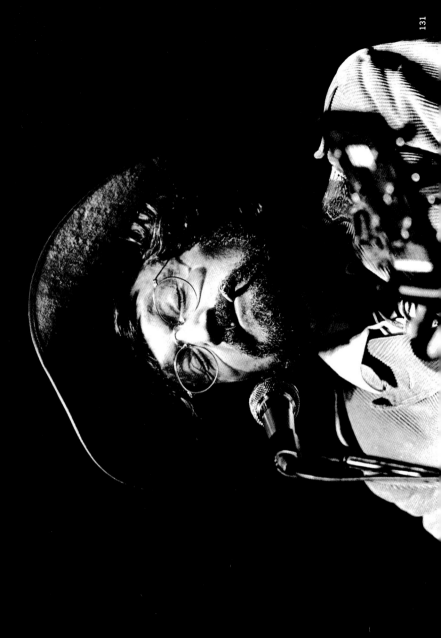

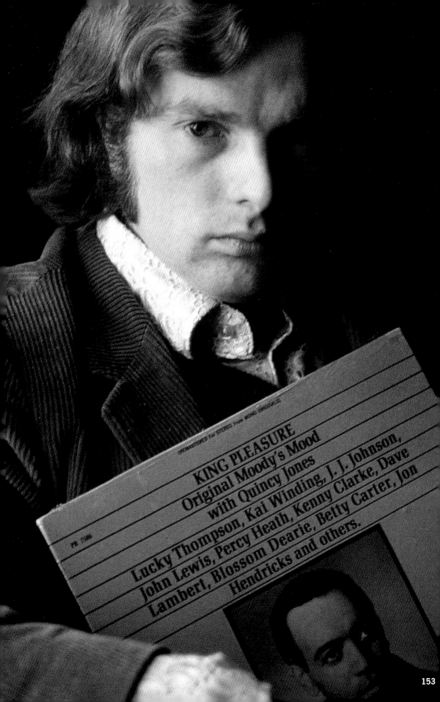

KING PLEASURE
Original Moody's Mood
with Quincy Jones
Lucky Thompson, Kai Winding, J. J. Johnson,
John Lewis, Percy Heath, Kenny Clarke, Dave
Lambert, Blossom Dearie, Betty Carter, Jon
Hendricks and others.

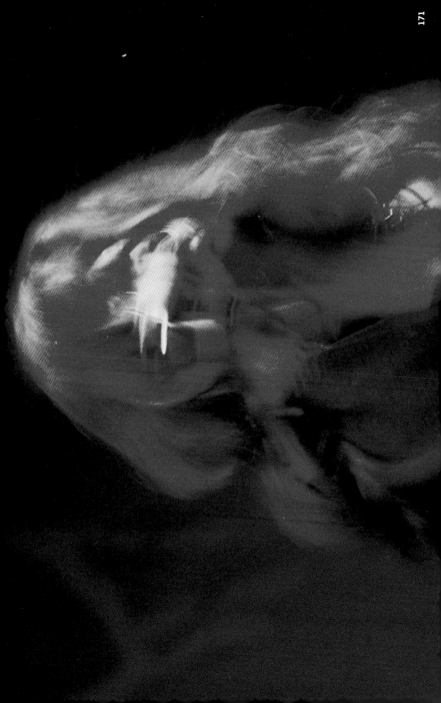

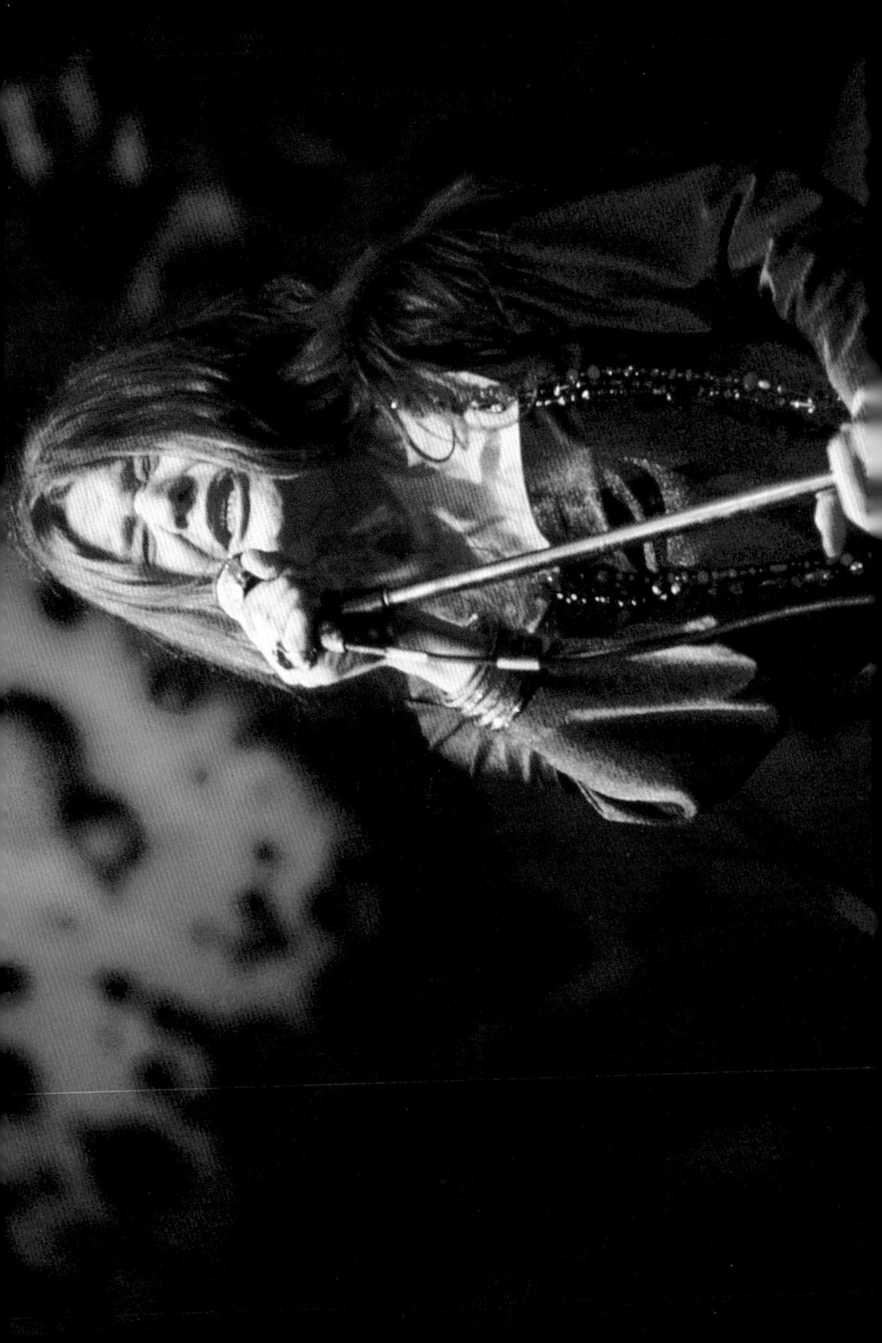

189

213

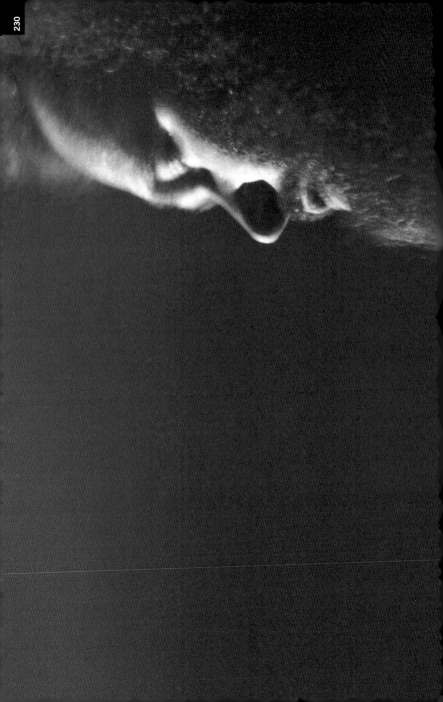

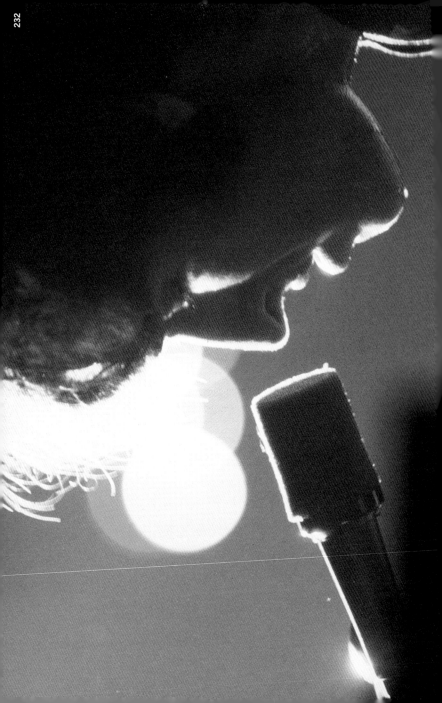

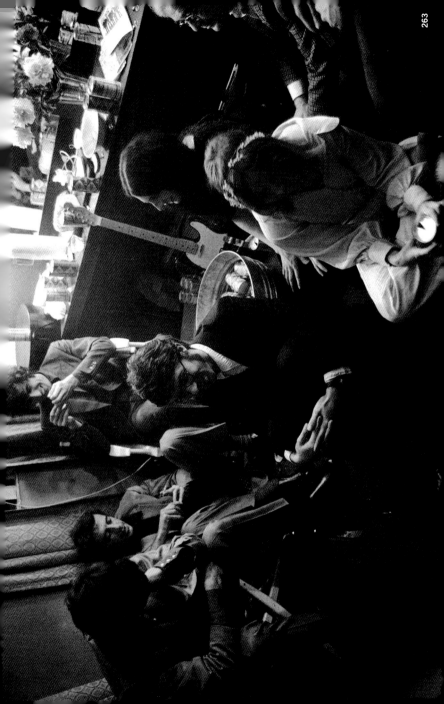

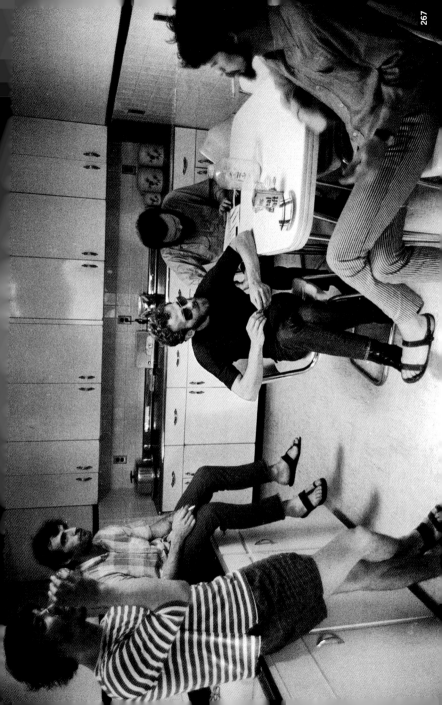

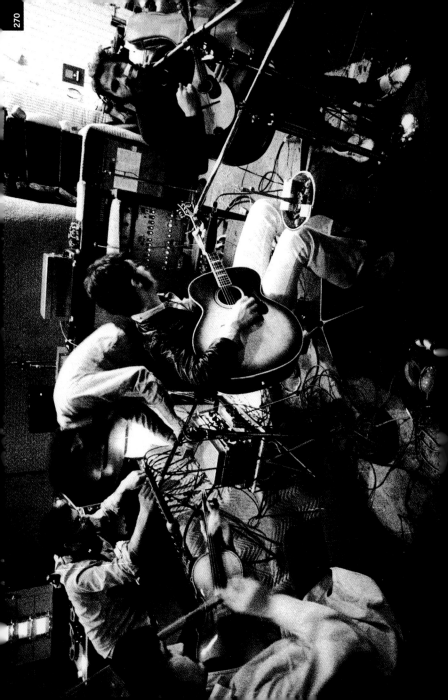

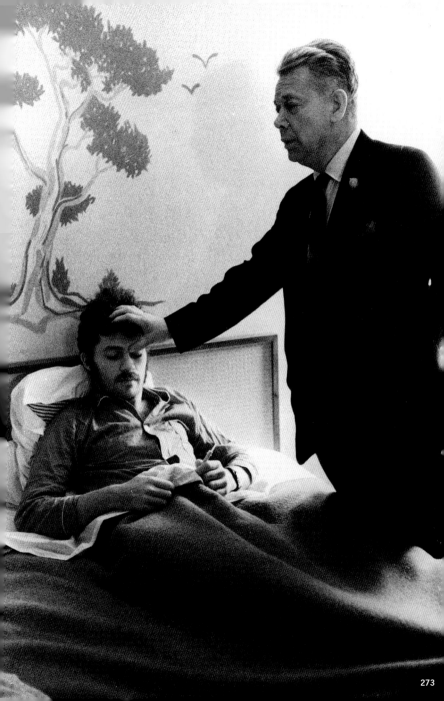

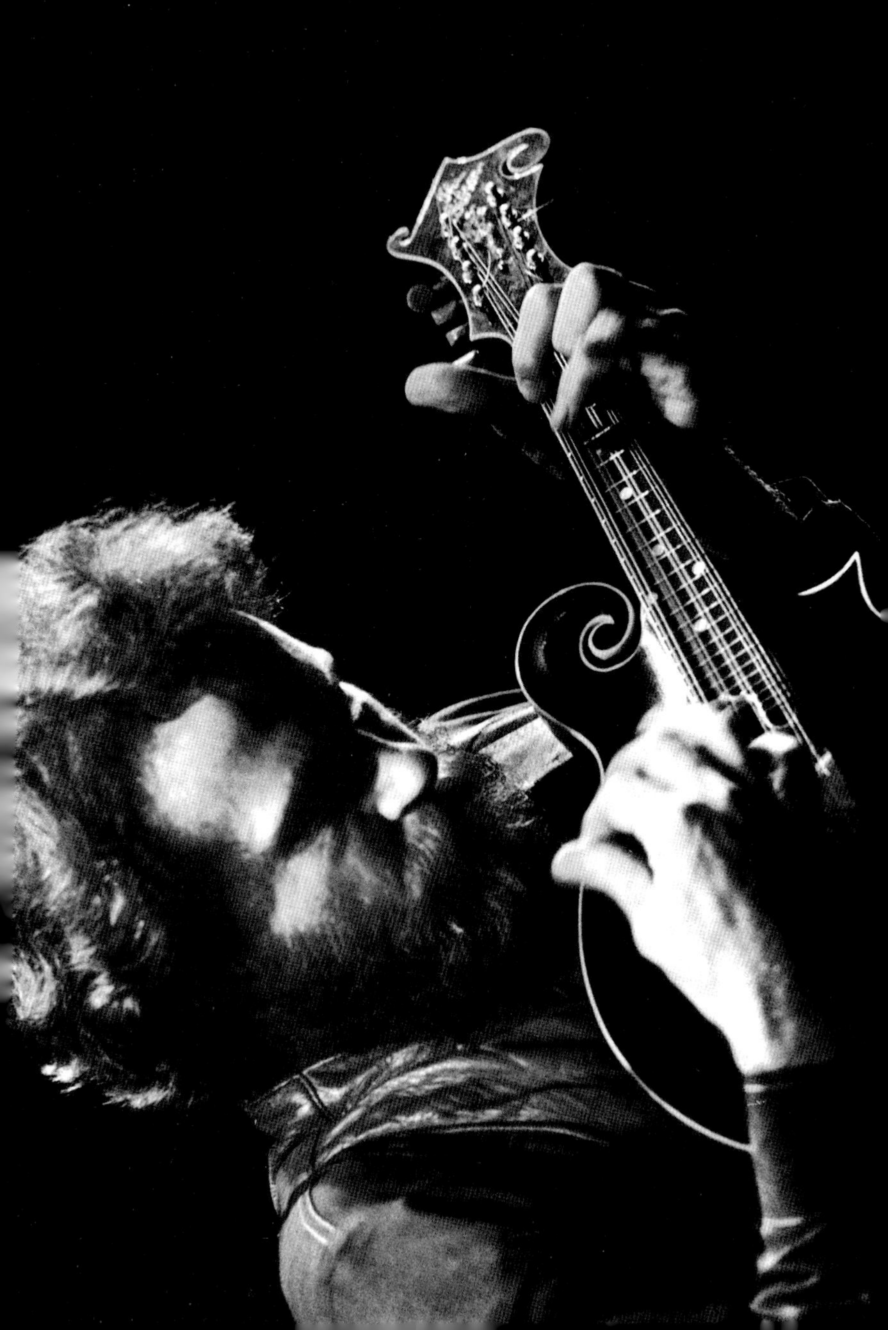

337

347

351

Biography / Biografie

Elliott Landy was born in New York in 1942. His first professional assignment was in 1967, when he went to Copenhagen to take photographs for a Danish film directed by Henning Carlsen featuring the famous Swedish actress Harriet Anderson. This was the first time Landy's work reached the public in a big way – his photographs appeared on the front pages of all the leading Danish and Swedish newspapers and magazines.

Towards the end of 1967 he returned to New York to join the protest movement against the Vietnam war. Working as a photographer and photo editor for underground newspapers, he took photographs at demonstrations for peace and social justice.

At the same time he started taking a series of celebrity shots at parties, producing a bizarre and highly amusing collection of photos that revealed some of the more unfamiliar characteristics of the stars of stage and screen. Of course Landy also devoted a lot of time to the Rock'n'Roll music scene, which was an integral part of the underground culture in the Sixties.

The photos of rock stars on stage and behind the scenes between 1967 and 1969 are his most important work. His pictures of Bob Dylan, The Band, Janis Joplin, Jimi Hendrix, Jim Morrison, Joan Baez, Van Morrison, Richie Havens and many others are a vivid documentation of the music scene during the classic period of rock music, which reached its zenith with the Woodstock festival in 1969, for which Landy was an official photographer.

In the early Seventies, Landy had had enough of taking photographs of musicians and concerts. He returned to Europe to seek out the roots of his inspiration, taking photographs of motifs in which he discovered beauty. Sometimes these were certain moments of his family life and his children. He spent the early part of his seven years in Europe hitchhiking, then traveled through ten different countries in a converted bus with forty seats. During this time photographs of his family were printed in the leading European newspapers. This was, so to speak, his second career.

In 1977 he returned to the United States and began working on interactive, visual films set to music, using the film camera as only a photographer can. He sold the results to nightclubs as background videos.

The end of the Eighties marked the beginning of his „impressionist" period, featuring a series of flower photographs whose style reminds us of this painting genre, without imitating it. For his New York photographs he also uses kaleidoscope lenses. He continues working in this style whenever the opportunity arises.

Since the end of 1997 he has been living with his new wife. The birth of his daughter inspired him to produce an extremely naturalistic black- and-white picture series on motherhood and feminine beauty – breast-feeding, nudes, cheerful childhood scenes.

For many years his photographs have been printed all over the world, on the front pages of „Rolling Stone", „Life" and the „Saturday Evening Post" and in countless European magazines. His music pictures have appeared on album covers, on the front covers of calendars, photo volumes, etc. He has also published a book and a CD-ROM entitled *Woodstock Vision. The Spirit of a Generation* and is the editor of the book *Woodstock 69. The First Festival.* At the moment he is working on the publication of a limited series of lithographs of his classic rock photos. He is also producing a film inspired by the life of Janis Joplin.

Elliott Landy wurde im Jahre 1942 in New York geboren. Seine erste professionelle Arbeit geht auf das Jahr 1967 zurück, als er in Kopenhagen für einen dänischen Film fotografierte, der unter der Regie von Henning Carlsen unter Mitwirkung der berühmten schwedischen Schauspielerin Harriet Anderson gedreht wurde. Dies ist Landys erste wirklich große öffentliche Arbeit: seine Fotoaufnahmen wurden von den wichtigsten dänischen und schwedischen Zeitschriften und Illustrierten als Titelbild verwendet.

Gegen Ende 1967 kehrte er nach New York zurück, um sich an den Protestbewegungen gegen den Vietnam-Krieg zu beteiligen. Während seiner Arbeit als Fotograf und Fotoeditor für Underground-Zeitschriften machte er auf Demonstrationen für Frieden und soziale Gerechtigkeit Aufnahmen.

Gleichzeitig machte er auf Partys Bilderserien von Prominenten, bei denen es ihm gelang, weniger bekannte Charaktereigenschaften von Stars des Films und der Bühne in einer bizarren, sehr humorvollen Fotosammlung zu erfassen. In den sechziger Jahren war die Musikszene des Rock'n'Roll integrierter Bestandteil der Underground-Kultur, und Landy widmete sich auch intensiv diesem Thema.

Seine Fotografien über das Musikleben jedoch, die er zwischen 1967 und 1969 von Rockstars auf der Bühne und hinter den Kulissen gemacht hat, stellen den bekanntesten Teil seiner Arbeit dar. Seine Bilder von Bob Dylan, The Band, Janis Joplin, Jimi Hendrix, Jim Morrison, Joan Baez, Van Morrison, Richie Havens und vielen anderen dokumentierten die Musikszene während der klassischen Periode des Rock, deren Höhepunkt 1969 das Woodstock-Festival darstellte, dessen offizieller Fotograf Landy war.

In den frühen siebziger Jahren war es Landy leid, Fotos von Musikern und Konzerten zu machen. Er kehrte nach Europa zurück, um hier die Wurzeln seiner Inspiration zu pflegen und Objekte zu fotografieren, in denen er Schönheit fand, die er auch in Momenten seines Familienlebens und den Bildern seiner Kinder suchte. Während der sieben Jahre in Europa, in denen er anfänglich als Anhalter und später in zehn europäischen Ländern an Bord eines umgebauten Busses mit vierzig Sitzen lebte und reiste, publizierte Landy in den wichtigsten europäischen Zeitschriften Fotografien seiner Familienmitglieder. Dies war sozusagen seine zweite Karriere.

1977 kehrte er in die Vereinigten Staaten zurück und begann mit der Arbeit an interaktiven, visuellen und musikalisch unterlegten Verfilmungen, wozu er einen für Fotografen typischen Filmaufnahmeapparat verwendete; das Material verkaufte er dann an Nachtklubs in Form von Ausstattungsvideos.

Gegen Ende der achtziger Jahre begann seine „impressionistische" Schaffensperiode, aus der eine Fotoserie von Blumen hervorging, die stilistisch an Malerei erinnert, ohne sie jedoch zu imitieren. Für seine Fotografien von New York benutzte er auch Kaleidoskoplinsen. So oft er in seinem Leben dazu Gelegenheit hatte, setzte er diesen Stil fort.

Von Ende 1997 an lebte er mit seiner neuen Frau; die Geburt seiner Tochter inspirierte ihn zu einer extrem naturalistischen Schwarz-Weiß-Reportage über die Mutterschaft und über die weibliche Schönheit: Stillen, Nackte, heitere Bilder der Kindheit.

Viele Jahre lang sind seine Fotografien auf der ganzen Welt publiziert worden, sei es auf den Titelseiten von „Rolling Stone", „Life", „Saturday Evening Post" usw., sei es in zahlreichen europäischen Magazinen. Seine Arbeiten über Musik erschienen auf Schallplattencovern, auf Deckblättern von Kalendern, Fotobänden usw. Außerdem veröffentlichte er *Woodstock Vision. The Spirit of a Generation* als Buch und CD-Rom und ist Herausgeber des Buches *Woodstock 69. The First Festival*. Zur Zeit ist er mit der Veröffentlichung einer limitierten Serie von Lithografien seiner klassischen Fotos über den Rock beschäftigt; darüber hinaus produziert er einen Film, zu dem er sich durch das Leben Janis Joplins inspirieren ließ.

Printed and bound
by Arti Grafiche Motta
Milan, Italy